SpringerBriefs in Cybersecurity

W0192901

For further volumes:
http://www.springer.com/series/10634

Cybersecurity is a difficult and complex field. The technical, political and legal questions surrounding it are complicated, often stretching a spectrum of diverse technologies, varying legal bodies, different political ideas and responsibilities. Cybersecurity is intrinsically interdisciplinary, and most activities in one field immediately affect the others. Technologies and techniques, strategies and tactics, motives and ideologies, rules and laws, institutions and industries, power and money—all of these topics have a role to play in cybersecurity, and all of these are tightly interwoven.

The SpringerBriefs in Cybersecurity series is comprised of two types of briefs: topic- and country-specific briefs. Topic-specific briefs strive to provide a comprehensive coverage of the whole range of topics surrounding cybersecurity, combining whenever possible legal, ethical, social, political and technical issues. Authors with diverse backgrounds explain their motivation, their mindset, and their approach to the topic, to illuminate its theoretical foundations, the practical nuts and bolts and its past, present and future. Country-specific briefs cover national perceptions and strategies, with officials and national authorities explaining the background, the leading thoughts and interests behind the official statements, to foster a more informed international dialogue.

Alana Maurushat

Disclosure of Security Vulnerabilities

Legal and Ethical Issues

 Springer

Alana Maurushat
Faculty of Law
The University of New South Wales
Sydney, NSW
Australia

ISSN 2193-973X   ISSN 2193-9748   (electronic)
ISBN 978-1-4471-5003-9   ISBN 978-1-4471-5004-6   (eBook)
DOI 10.1007/978-1-4471-5004-6
Springer London Heidelberg New York Dordrecht

Library of Congress Control Number: 2013932453

Printed on acid-free paper

Springer is part of Springer Science+Business Media (www.springer.com)

Foreword

Information is a critical corporate assert that has become vulnerable to attacks from viruses, hackers, criminals and human error. Consequently organisations have to prioritise the security of their computer systems. With the abundance of information that an organisation must protect and with identity theft at an all-time high, security has never been as important as it is today for business and individuals.

The speed at which technology is changing makes for the never-ending creation of new vulnerabilities. At the same time, these same technologies also facilitate better-crafted and more effective attacks. While software vendors are reducing the number of known vulnerabilities, hackers are improving their abilities to get around previously available defences. Because of this, organisations and individuals must be equipped with the knowledge of how information divulged could precipitate further attacks and compromise their states of systems. Managing these vulnerabilities has become a critical component in the protection of the citizens and consumers.

Disclosure is one of the main contentious topics in computer security. The great debate these days is whether or not those discovering security vulnerabilities should publicise them through full disclosure or keep the problems private and unspoken. Opinions vary on whether security researchers and other stakeholders should go public with software flaws or data breaches early. At one end of the spectrum are the proponents of full disclosure who contend that by publicly announcing vulnerabilities, security professionals can begin to mitigate the associated risks and to compel developers to develop a patch to fix the flaw promptly. Secrecy will encourage vendors to procrastinate on fixing the problems or may decide to do nothing. Thus, public scrutiny is the only reliable way to improve security. Others counter that the risk of exploitation is likely to be greater when the vulnerability is made public. The information given to the public may allow criminals to reverse engineer the vulnerability. Defenders of "secrecy" argue that vendors and organisations must be given a head start to diagnose and fix the flaw before going public with the information. At the middle of the spectrum are those who claim that disclosure fell in between.

The problem on how vulnerabilities are managed and disclosed is further complicated by the different legal and regulatory regimes. While discovering and publishing vulnerabilities are generally legal, sometimes laws have been passed to suppress research on security. Researchers have either been issued injunctions from disclosing the vulnerabilities or prosecuted. The legal and ethical issues around the disclosure of security vulnerabilities are best described as a legal landmine.

Disclosure of Security Vulnerabilities considers both ethical and legal issues involved with the disclosure of vulnerabilities and looks at the ways in which law might respond to these challenges. The key objective is to fill a gap in existing literature on legal and ethical dimensions by providing readers with a comprehensive source of latest trends, cases, issues and research in this field. Written by Alana Maurushat, co-director of Cyberspace Law and Policy Center at the Faculty of Law of the University of New South Wales in Australia, this book raises a number of pressing issues that organisations and individuals are facing today concerning the management of security vulnerabilities. She cuts through the legal jargon and discusses legal issues and topics in a straightforward way. It is a rare skill, but is one deployed through this thoughtful book.

I am pleased to be able to recommend this book to readers who are looking for substantive materials on the aspect of managing information security or looking to understand the important aspects of information security disclosures. Disclosure of Security Vulnerabilities is an excellent reference book.

Sylvia Kierkegaard

Acknowledgments

The author wishes to thank the editing and production staff at Springer, and Professors Graham Greenleaf and Roger Clarke for their careful reading and recommendations of parts of this monograph. I also wish to thank the student interns at the Cyberspace Law and Policy Centre for their diligence, research and raw enthusiasm given to all things "cyber". Lastly, I wish to thank my researchers Eliss Kong and Lauren Loz.

Contents

Chapter 1
Introduction

Abstract Much debate has been given to whether computer security is improved through full disclosure of security vulnerabilities versus keep the problems private and unspoken. Although there is still tension between those who feel strongly about the subject, a middle ground of responsible disclosure seems to have emerged. Unfortunately, just as we've moved into an era with more responsible disclosure, it would seem that there is a growing market for security vulnerabilities and zero day exploits. This book considers both ethical and legal issues involved with the disclosure of vulnerabilities and looks at the ways in which law might respond to these challenges.

1.1 Painting the Computer Security Landscape

If one could paint a picture of the state of computer security it would look like this:

Painting courtesy of Francoise Matz

A. Maurushat, *Disclosure of Security Vulnerabilities*, SpringerBriefs in Cybersecurity, DOI: 10.1007/978-1-4471-5004-6_1, © The Author(s) 2013

Before the observer is an abstract painting with a mixture of variant tones of red and black with light use of yellow and orange. A white canvas acquires colour, texture and depth one layer at a time. A mesh screen of rows and columns is screened over the top of the white canvas after black paint has been applied to the screen producing a grid or matrix-like appearance of black squares. The pressure and amount of paint applied determines the intensity of the black for each square. This is the initial infrastructure. At this point, the artist will add colour, shape and contour to the now matrix-like canvas. In this case, the artist has added concentrated reds with more subtle oranges and yellows. In one sense, the art becomes a reaction to what is already there. The difficulty lies in knowing when to put away the brush in order to achieve a creation of balance and harmonized composition; the temptation to keep adding colour and contour is compelling.

Images courtesy of Francoise Matz and Catharine MacIntosh

Now imagine this image being painted by many artists, each contributing a portion of work with minimal communication between them. Upon closer examination of the work you will see a pattern of random, and almost invisible, tiny holes. The end result of this anarchic collaboration is a compelling piece of art perforated with weaknesses, some visible, most invisible. You now have a representation of computer security. The initial white canvas covered in a grid is the basic technological infrastructure often referred to as the 'physical' layer comprised of wires, routers, and switches.[1] Each

---

[1] [1]. There are two competing models which dominate Internet analysis. The first is the Open Systems Interconnection Basic Reference Model (OSI Model) which is comprised of seven layers: physical, data link, network, transport, session, presentation and application. *See* http://www.en.wikipedia.org/wiki/OSI_model. The other model is the TCP/IP Model which has five layers: application, transport, network, data link and physical. *See* http://www.en.wikipedia.org/wiki/TCP/IP_model.

stroke of the colour red represents a secure technical application on the Internet.[2] All other colours represent predictable and known security vulnerabilities to the *technical community* though a significant portion of *users* remain unable to spot the scant portions of yellow, others are unable to differentiate between various hues of orange and red while another portion of users are colour-blind. The tiny perforations or holes represent a different set of security vulnerabilities. These vulnerabilities are often unnoticed. Some go unnoticed by the technical community. Many are unnoticed by governing entities. Most if not all are unnoticed by users, both commercial and home consumers.

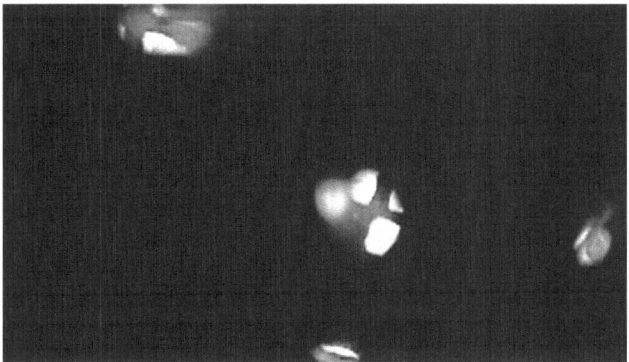

Courtesy of Catharine MacIntosh

Without a magnifying glass or the opportunity to view the painting close-up, the tiny holes are unobserved. Even then it is impossible to know which holes have been placed deliberately by the artist, which holes are unwanted defacements, and which holes have been caused purely by accident. Paint is lost through these holes in the same way that information seeps through unwanted channels to undesirable recipients. This is the state of play of Computer Security—a chaotic mess.

Much computer software is inherently insecure and there is a need to take responsibility for producing more software with less severe vulnerabilities. Software liability is deeply enmeshed in a long political debate with strong lobbyist protection of the industry.[3] One method of improving security is to sue those in a position to prevent attacks such as software and hardware developers that produce insecure products. Software and hardware companies are shielded from most forms of consumer protection law through warranty clauses. It has been argued that there is little incentive for software and hardware companies to produce secure products.[4] The blatant insecurity of some software and hardware does not sit well with many computer software programmers, including hackers. The computer

---

[2] Libicki refers to this as the 'syntactic layer' which is comprised of instruction and interaction between information systems. This is also known as the 'application layer'. *Refer to* Note 1, p. 8.

[3] *See generally* [2].

[4] Scholars such as Jennifer Chandler and Meiring de Villiers have written on tort liability for insecure software. *See* [3, 4]. *See also* an economic model for software liability in [5].

security disclosure movement is in many ways a response to the state of insecurity of software and hardware, and it is hoped that such disclosure of vulnerabilities will provide incentive for the industry to produce better products. The issue of security vulnerability disclosure remains a constant source of discourse amongst the computer security industry, with firmly held beliefs from all sides.

1.1.1 Research Method

For the purpose of clarity, the conventional computer security model is used in this book. Under the model, threats impinge on vulnerabilities to cause harm. Safeguards are used to prevent or ameliorate that harm. More specifically:

- A **threat** is a circumstance that could result in harm, and may be natural, accidental or intentional. A party *directly* responsible for an intentional threat is referred to as an attacker;
- **Harm** is anything that has deleterious consequences, and includes injury to persons, damage to property, financial loss, loss of value of an asset, and loss of reputation and confidence;
- A **vulnerability** is a feature or weakness that gives rise to a susceptibility of a threat;
- An **exploit** is an attack on a computer system that takes advantage of a vulnerability that the system offers to attackers. "Used as a verb, the term refers to the act of successfully making such an attack"[5]
- A **safeguard** is a measure intended to avoid or reduce vulnerabilities.

In a typical scenario there is a vulnerability in a piece of software or hardware. An attacker may discover the vulnerability on his/her own then choose to exploit the vulnerability resulting in a threat. Alternatively the attacker may discover the vulnerability due to the fact that another has published it and therefore made it known to a wider audience. The attacker then exploits the vulnerability resulting in a threat which may or may not lead to harm.

Vulnerabilities and threats fall into three broad categories:

- **Known vulnerability** is a feature or weakness that has been made public through some form of communication, often publication;
- A **zero day exploit** "is one that takes advantage of a security vulnerability on the same day that the vulnerability becomes generally known. There are zero days between the time the vulnerability is discovered and the first attack." It also entails exploits of unknown vulnerabilities and not just recently published ones;[6] or
- A **future threat** is a circumstance that could result in harm as the result of a previously unknown security vulnerability.

---

[5] Rouse M "Exploit" at http://searchsecurity.techtarget.com/definition/exploit.

[6] Rouse M "Zero Day Exploit" at http://searchsecurity.techtarget.com/definition/zero-day-exploit.

Whether a threat or vulnerability is "disclosed" depends on whether and in the manner of which it is published. Publication can be partial or full. For example, a party may discuss a vulnerability in a piece of software or hardware using vague references or by only revealing parts of the vulnerability. In order to take advantage of the vulnerability the attacker would have to discover the missing links on their own. As the remainder of the Chapters will reveal, whether there is legal liability and possible criminal sanction are dependent on a number of factors including:

- whether or not a vulnerability is published;
- whether the publication is partial or full;
- publication venue; and
- recipients of publication.

Not only do the above factors contribute to a legal position, they also point to ethical issues in disclosure (responsible disclosure). As will be illustrated in Chaps. 4 and 5, the disclosure of security vulnerabilities is a risky proposition from a legal perspective in that both criminal charges and civil liability may ensue.

1.1.2 Disclosure Movements

The inherent state of poor software and hardware security prompted two movements with competing philosophies on disclosure of security vulnerabilities. The first is what is known as "security through obscurity". This was the industry line toted by computer security experts or white hat hackers. Security holes, vulnerabilities/bugs, and attack methods are kept private; these vulnerabilities were known only amongst a small group of "trusted" security experts. It was believed that by keeping the known security vulnerabilities or bugs a secret, that no one will be able to find the vulnerabilities and then exploit them.

The computer security community is comprised of many sub-communities. These sub-communities have taken different positions on their views towards disclosure. For example, in cryptography, "security through obscurity" became to be considered as undesirable when Kerckhoff's Principle—assuming that everything about a crypto-system is known by the enemy, the system should still be constructed so that it remains secure—was published in 1883 in "La cryptographie militaire".[7]

The anti-virus community has up until very recently held fast to the notion of closed security. Closed security borrows from "security through obscurity" in that there is a similar notion that vulnerabilities if shared at all, should only be shared amongst a small group of trusted entities. Another movement, however, began to take hold in the late 1990s. This was the "full disclosure" movement which paralleled the open source software movement. The "full disclosure" concept is also referred to as "open security".

---

[7] Reproduced in Peticolas F "La cryptography militaire." An English version is also available on Peticolas' website at http://petitcolas.net/fabien/kerckhoffs/.

The open source software movement posed a profound challenge to the way that software was made and distributed. Projects were established and programmers communicated and contributed software building blocks to one another via the Internet. When a software program was completed by this method, it was then generally offered to the public over the Internet, sometimes free of charge, but always free of the use restrictions common to most software.[8] The open source movement was more than a user-developer model of software development; it had evolved into a culture with its own customs, traditions and expectations. It has been described as a "community of people as a locus of innovation, where knowledge, practice, and technological artefacts are interdependent parts of an evolving social system".[9] Others have characterised the open source community as a "gift culture".[10] In gift cultures, social status is determined not by what you control but by what you give away. Open source programmers are proud to extol what they believe to be a superior method of software development. It has been argued, for example, that open source projects produce better quality technology than traditional corporate research and development.[11] The open source model operates on the premise that, by having the opportunity to build on each other's ideas, rather than duplicate one another's efforts in a "closed" system, software developers are able to produce more efficient and technologically superior products. This efficiency and superiority stemmed from a few basic principles as expressed by open source guru Eric Raymond: many heads are better than one, and people are most motivated when they are personally interested in the work. An open source project employs the Internet as its means of making the source code available attracting a potentially unlimited amount of co-developers. These co-developers are able to look at the code, improve it, make suggestions, locate bugs, debug, and so forth much more rapidly than in a "closed" system.

The "full disclosure" or "open security" movement echoed many themes as seen in the open source movement. Open security advocates believed that the discussion of security problems with a wide audience would expedite fixing the vulnerabilities, and that such discussion not only advanced security as a whole but also hacking in general. In this instance, hacker refers to "A person who delights in having an intimate understanding of the internal workings of a system, computers and computer networks in particular. The term is often misused in a pejorative context, where "cracker" would be the correct term".[12] As cyber security journalist Kevin Poulsen writes in his book about the infamous real life hacker, Max Butler, hackers believed that, "Keeping bugs private only benefited two groups: the bad guys who were

---

[8] *See* Stallman R "What is Free Software" found on http://www.gnu.org/philosophy/free-sw.html.

[9] [6].

[10] Raymond E *The Cathedral and the Bazaar: Musings on Linux and Open Source by an Accidental Revolutionary* (Sebastapol: O'Reily & Associates, R'vd Ed., 2001).

[11] Raymond, above.

[12] RFC 1392 Internet Users Glossary.

exploiting them, and vendors like Microsoft that preferred to fix security holes without confessing the details of their screwups".[13]

Full disclosure mailing lists, and discussion boards popped up in the 1990s where disciples sent in details of software and hardware security flaws. Some disclosure forums adhered to policies where the software maker would be notified of the vulnerability, and given the opportunity to fix the bug before the flaw was released to the mailing list or discussion board. Other mailing lists and discussion boards such as Bugtraq simply posted a previously unknown vulnerability or bug to the mailing list without notifying the software maker of the problem. The industry practice has been to patch the vulnerability once notified or patch the vulnerability at a later time. The lack of immediate or reasonable response time between a vendor becoming aware of the problem and then patching the vulnerability became a strong incentive to simply make the vulnerability known without first communicating with the vendor. The vulnerability would be made known instantly to thousands of security experts, both hackers, security experts/white hat hackers, and crackers/black hat hackers alike.

While there remains some tension between closed security/security through obscurity and open security/full disclosure advocates, the pendulum is swinging towards open security. There is less argument about the benefits and detriments of no disclosure versus full disclosure, with emphasis being placed on responsible disclosure. In particular, technology companies see value in inviting hackers to identify vulnerabilities in their systems. Companies such as Google, Microsoft and Sony now routinely organise and run hacking competitions of their products.[14] There are also bounty programs whereby organisations pay for both exploit information, as well as information leading to the source of the exploit.[15] Other more conventional companies outside of the technology realm, have been slower to see open security as a benefit. In spite of the gain in momentum and acceptance of the open security principle, security researchers are not immune to criminal provisions and legal liability for disclosure of security vulnerabilities.

Open disclosure potentially allows for vulnerabilities to be found and fixed in a more efficient manner. It also allows for the possibility of vulnerabilities being fixed before an exploit is used for some malicious purpose such as intellectual property theft or fraud. It is also thought that open disclosure incentivises companies to more quickly patch vulnerabilities. On the downside, open disclosure potentially makes vulnerabilities public knowledge for anyone to see, and take advantage of. The publication of a zero day exploit to the public or presented at a hacking conference allows people to take advantage of the vulnerability for nefarious purposes. Indeed, there is empirical work suggesting that security attack frequency increases after vulnerability disclosure.[16]

---

[13] [7].

[14] See hacking competitions run by vendors as http://blog.chromium.org/2012/08/announcing-pwnium-2.html.

[15] See for example the Google bounty program available at http://www.google.com/about/appsecurity/reward-program.

[16] [8].

Computer security vulnerabilities are disclosed in a variety of ways. Disclosure may be by a third party, self-disclosure, or by accident. Methods of discovery of security vulnerabilities include honeynets and other observation of data traffic, reverse engineering, hacking forums and blogs, youtube proof of concept videos, public conferences, security experts and CERTs alerts, by hacking, and internal and external audits. Vulnerabilities are varied and may include weakness in software and hardware. The vulnerability may also be as simple as listing a location of an unpatched PC, or a PC running insecure software in order to gain access into a system, or a vulnerable point of sale device. Vulnerabilities are disclosed by professional security organisations such as the CERTs or the Anti-Phishing Working Party, or by crackers to share information for malicious purpose such as identity theft or fraud (often credit card fraud). Parties also have varied motivations to disclose vulnerabilities including the promotion of better security, blackmail, anticensorship, competition between rival software or hardware companies, political motivation, and in order to comply with disclosure regulations.

The legal and ethical issues around the disclosure of security vulnerabilities might best be described as a legal landmine. There is a paucity of legal cases dealing directly with the issue. This may in part be due to the fact that many problems have been settled without the need to prosecute or pursue in civil action. As many security disclosures are published anonymously and/or with the use of anonymising technologies making traceback to the original discloser difficult, whether laws might apply to a situation is somewhat moot. Nonetheless, there are still many situations where the law could be applied for security disclosure, or failing to disclose a security breach. And while the application of such laws to open security may be a grey zone, it is also an emerging area therefore it is difficult to stare into the future to predict if there will be political will to extend the reach of the law to such disclosures, or whether to shy away from using law as a solution.

References

1. Libicki M (2007) National security and information warfare. Cambridge University Press, Cambridge
2. Rice D (2008) Geekonomics: the real cost of insecure software. Addison-Wesley, Reading
3. Chandler J (2006) Liability for Botnet attacks. Can J Law Technol
4. Chandler J (2003–2004) Security in cyberspace: combating distributed denial of service attacks. Univ Ottawa Law Technol J 231
5. de Villiers M (2009) Information security standards. University of New South Wales Law Research Paper Working Paper 34
6. Tuomi I (2001) Internet, innovation, and open source: actors in the network. Available on http://www.firstmonday.dk/issues/issue6_1/tuomi
7. Poulsen K (2011) Kingpin: the true story of Max Butler, the master Hacker who ran a billion dollar cyber crime network. Hachette, Australia, p 42
8. Arora A, Nandkumar A, Telang R (2006) Does information security attack frequency increase with vulnerability disclosure? An empirical analysis Spring Science & Business Media. DOI 10.1007/s10796-006-9012-5

Chapter 2
Types of Disclosure

Abstract While there are many different types of vulnerability disclosure, two broad categories cover most situations. These are third party disclosure and self-disclosure. This chapter looks at a variety of motivations for each of these broad disclosure categories and draws on case studies where possible to provide context and as a means for introducing legal discussion. More detailed legal and ethical discussion is found in Chaps. 4 and 5.

2.1 Introduction

This chapter examines the main types of disclosure of security vulnerabilities drawing on third party disclosures and self-disclosures as well as motivating factors to disclose. A variety of case studies will be used to highlight the different elements involved with techniques. Legal and ethical issues of such disclosures are explored in later chapters.

2.1.1 Third Party Disclosure

A third party disclosure is when a party who is not the author, owner or rights holder of a piece of software, hardware, or other aspect of a data system, publishes the information of a vulnerability. Motivations for disclosure are varied.

2.1.1.1 In Good Faith to Promote Better Security Practices

Penetration/Intrusion Testing is a type of information systems security testing on behalf of the system's owners. This is known in the computer security world as "ethical hacking". There is some argument, however, as to whether penetration

A. Maurushat, *Disclosure of Security Vulnerabilities*, SpringerBriefs in Cybersecurity,
DOI: 10.1007/978-1-4471-5004-6_2, © The Author(s) 2013

testing must be done with permission from a system's owner or whether a benevolent intention would suffice in the absence of permission.[1] Whether permission is obtained or not does not change the common cause, that of improving security.

Most penetration or intrusion testing occurs when a security expert is hired to test the security of an organisation's network. In this sense, the security expert has permission to hack into the organisation's network such that the law will view this as authorised, thereby not attracting criminal sanction. The legal ambiguity arises when these same security experts stumble across security vulnerabilities, then actively investigates further without permission or authorisation from the system's owner. It is only this latter form of act which would be considered as legally and morally ambiguous.

Security Activism is similar to penetration/intrusion testing in that the cause is to improve security. Security activism may go beyond mere testing of security, however, to gather intelligence on attackers, and to launch active attacks to disrupt criminal online enterprises. And in many instances, security activism involves the discovery of vulnerabilities and the disclosure of such vulnerabilities with the aspiration of improving security.

Case Study: First State Superannuation Vulnerability

In 2011, an Australian security expert Patrick Webster was threatened with legal action and criminal charges for disclosing a serious security flaw in First State's Superannuation System.[2] When Webster went to log into the First State system to check on his superannuation he noticed that the URL contained his individual identity information linking to his superannuation account. He found this odd, and to investigate further, Patrick ran a simple for loop script to check for other anomalies. The script started with the scan of one account number then continued to scan by incremented numbers. In the time that it took to initialise the script (computer program), make tea and come back to the computer, the script revealed hundreds of megabytes of account data. Upon seeing this, Patrick ascertained that potentially every account was exposed to the Internet. He quit running the program. In the scanning time, the script automatically saved the details of the first 500 accounts.[3]

Alarmed at this security flaw, Webster notified the information technology personnel at First State Superannuation. Some of the IT staff sent him emails thanking him.[4] However, the Chief Information Officer and others at First State Superannuation reacted differently alleging that by accessing not just his own

---

[1] [1]

[2] Greenberg, above.

[3] Webster, above.

[4] See footnote 3.

account but the accounts of others he had committed a crime. Webster was served with legal papers and was told that the police might press charges against him. What is more alarming is the fact this security flaw should have been picked up through basic security compliance checks. It is further alarming that over 770,000 FSS accounts were vulnerable, as well as the details of another 1.2 million accounts from other companies who outsourced their data storage to Pillar Administration.[5] The alarming rate of corporations having their data compromised has sparked data breach notification laws around the globe yet corporations and organisations still have not implemented many basic security mechanisms (data breach notification is explored in Chap. 5). First State Superannuation is reviewing its data storage contract with Pillar as well as its own personal handling of personal information.

It has become standard industry practice to thank and often reward those individuals who alert companies to security flaws. Corporations such as Facebook and Google send their thanks and offer a small reward. Anti-virus and anti-spyware companies also pay money for zero day threats. In this instance, however, First State's reaction was to threaten Webster with civil and criminal proceedings if he didn't turn his computer over to the IT personnel at First State for them to verify that he had deleted the information from those 500 accounts.[6] The charges were later dropped. This incident has set off alarm bells for security researchers in Australia and perhaps even abroad.

In the words of Patrick Webster:

> I am genuinely disappointed the government legislation will not provide safeguards for security researchers, though I am not the least bit surprised.

> I've encountered clients who are actively being attacked by a compromised legitimate website and considered counter attacking in self defence to protect my client and the compromised organisation… I haven't, but it would be nice if we could.

> My only hope is that my incident with First State Superannuation sets a precedent for future researchers…. with any luck the media attention will convince corporations that not everybody is acting with malicious intent. If it helps just one researcher in the future I'll be happy.[7]

The incident is a reminder that even though Patrick engaged in responsible security disclosure by approaching the company first in order for them to fix the bug, this did not exempt him from the reach of the law. In the end a lack of political will to prosecute coupled with some undesirable media attention on First State Insurance won out. This incident is also a timely reminder of the lack of legitimate exemptions for security research which will be discussed in Chap. 4.

---

[5] [2].

[6] Discussion with Patrick Webster.

[7] Email correspondence with Patrick Webster.

2.1.1.2 Malicious Intent to Profit Financially from Vulnerability

Illegitimate exploit markets are aimed at financial profit. In an exploit market scenario, someone discovers a vulnerability or an exploit. They contact the potentially affected owner and demand a fee in exchange for them not to publish or reveal the exploit. Such exploits might also be considered theoretically as blackmail or extortion, but, as will be seen, such exploit markets operate within the law. Similar tactics are used in denial of service attacks. Pay me a fee or I will attack your website. Though in the case of threat to launch a denial of service attack, the event is illegal as a form of blackmail or extortion. The motivation in denial of service attacks and selling exploits is financial, and the techniques used are largely similar, one is considered legal and the other illegal, yet both remain unethical.

Exploits and vulnerabilities are also exchanged in hacking forums. This can be done merely as an act of courtesy to share in the goods. The exchange of exploits is also done as a favour or in exchange of information amongst attackers. Exploits and vulnerabilities can be sold on the black market to those wanting to use the exploit or vulnerability for nefarious purposes.

The terms darknet and blackmarkets are often used interchangeably. A darknet is an isolated network from the Internet that is used to share or exchange files.[8] Many items are exchanged in a darknet including music, movie files, credit card details, information, streams of data, as well as exploits. A darknet is thought of as a black market as many, but not all, darknets are illegal.

For example, in Kevin Poulsen's biography of the infamous darknet master, Max Butler, he describes the workings of darknets, and in particular describes the inner workings of two darknets: DarkMarket (DM) and Carders Market (CM).[9] DM and CM are just two of many different black market places to exchange and sell information, including exploits. Similar markets operate in non-English languages. Mazafucka is one Russian syndicate operating a darknet dealing with all types of illicit materials, including the sale of exploits.[10] The trade of exploits, as will be seen in the next section, is moving from a black market to an open market space.

The last decade has seen the birth of above ground (legitimate) exploit markets. An exploit market is a "place" where one is able to sell information (often zero day exploit) about a vulnerability or exploit to another party before the exploit is disclosed to the broader hacker community or likewise detected from the anti-virus software community. A clever hacker might discover a zero day exploit, he/she then either contacts the owner of the vulnerable product (Eg. Apple, Google, HP) and receives a fee for the discovery. Other exploit markets such as Zero Day Initiative and iDefense operate under a different model whereby the vulnerability

---

[8] See for example, "The Future of Darknets" (YouTube video looking at intellectual property) available at http://www.youtube.com/watch?v=m2cZ-t-kVKQ.

[9] Poulsen, footnote 13 in Chap. 1.

[10] [3].

is disclosed to the vendor for free as a marketing tool for their security products and services to protect the vendor.

In other contexts, middle man brokers have emerged on the scene as well as mercenary style corporations specialising in the discovery and sale of zero day exploits. Zero day exploits, can attract a figure ranging from $1,000 to a quarter of a million dollars.[11] Often a company such as Google or HP will hold a hacking competition of their product at security conferences. The discovery of the vulnerability(ies) enables the winner to collect a cash prize, and earn a reputation in the field which may lead to consultancies and other business opportunities. The example of a mercenary exploit-selling firm is considered below.

Case Study: Specialty Exploit-Selling Firms

Exploit specialty firms are on the rise. These firms specialise in discovering zero day exploits in products such as the IOS, Google Chrome, and so forth. These companies then either sell the exploit to the vendor (Eg. Google) in exchange for a fee often between $2,000 and $60,000. The exploit is disclosed only to the vendor.

Other firms such as the French exploit-selling Vupen are selling exploits to a group of customers as opposed to exclusive sales. In the case of controversial Vupen, the exploits are sold to governments around the world.[12] The company has been described as the "Jersey Shore of the exploit trade", "ethically challenged opportunists" and "modern-day merchant of death," selling "the bullets for cyber-war."[13] Vupen sells state of the art intrusion methods for software (and some hardware) where customers (typically governments) pay a subscription fee for a range of techniques made available for them to then utilise for whatever purpose they have in mind. For this reason, some industry players have compared them to arms dealers.[14]

In instance of professional exploit firms, full disclosures are made but only to a limited audience, either to an exclusive vendor or to a list of customers (governments). While the practice, particularly strong in the case of Vupen, is legal, it is difficult to see ethical virtue in the trade.

2.1.1.3 Political Motive

Not all disclosures and exploits are done in order to profit financially. The last five years has seen the explosion of hacktivism by movements such as Anonymous, LulzSec and 4Chan. In some of these incidents there were political motives behind

---

[11] [4].

[12] [5].

[13] Quotes by industry leaders in Greenberg [5].

[14] Greenberg see footnote 4.

varying releases of security disclosures. In these incidents vulnerabilities are disclosed as a form of payback or retribution, in addition to denial of service attacks and counter-denial of service attacks. One particularly interesting example is examined below.

Case Study: LulzSec Wikileaks Operation Payback

LulzSec is a group of computer hackers who attack targets and expose security vulnerabilities. In 2011 they released a manifesto after their 1,000th tweet where they claimed to be in it for the laughs and entertaining value. Equally, the manifesto points out that they are performing a good deed by improving computer security. As written in the manifesto:

> Do you think every hacker announces everything they've hacked? We certainly haven't, and we're damn sure others are playing the silent game. Do you feel safe with your Facebook accounts, your Google Mail accounts, your Skype accounts? What makes you think a hacker isn't silently sitting inside all of these right now, sniping out individual people, or perhaps selling them off? You are a peon to these people. A toy. A string of characters with a value.
>
> This is what you should be fearful of, not us releasing things publicly, but the fact that someone hasn't released something publicly. We're sitting on 200,000 Brink users right now that we never gave out. It might make you feel safe knowing we told you, so that Brink users may change their passwords. What if we hadn't told you? No one would be aware of this theft, and we'd have a fresh 200,000 peons to abuse, completely unaware of a breach.
>
> Yes, yes, there's always the argument that releasing everything in full is just as evil, what with accounts being stolen and abused, but welcome to 2011. This is the lulz lizard era, where we do things just because we find it entertaining. Watching someone's Facebook picture turn into a penis and seeing their sister's shocked response is priceless. Receiving angry emails from the man you just sent 10 dildos to because he can't secure his Amazon password is priceless. You find it funny to watch havoc unfold, and we find it funny to cause it. We release personal data so that equally evil people can entertain us with what they do with it."[15]

Some of LulzSec's latest attacks appear to be politically motivated. In a question and answer session with LulzSec member Whirlpool, he professed that "Politically motivated ethical hacking is more fulfilling".[16] A good example of politically motivated hacking and disclosure involves the Operation Payback attacks, and their aftermath.

Wikileaks founder Julian Assange was arrested in London in order to facilitate his extradition to Sweden where he is wanted on charges of sexual crime under Swedish law.[17] Many viewed this as a false arrest and indirect way of incarcerating Assange for the release of secret US cables to Wikileaks. A legal defence fund

---

[15] LulzSec—1,000th Tweet Statement http://pastebin.com/HZtH523f.

[16] [6].

[17] [7].

was quickly established where people could make donations via Mastercard or Paypal to help the cause. Mastercard and Paypal disallowed any payments to be made to the Assange legal defence fund causing an international uproar, and in particular, within hacktivism communities. Members of LulzSec launched a denial of service attack against Mastercard and Paypal which took down their capabilities in December 2010 and then again in June 2011. There was a denial and counter-denial of service attack showdown which might best be seen as gunfire between warring factions, with evidence that the US government contracted security firms to perform attacks against Wikileaks and other journalists.

Additionally, law enforcement were on the hunt for the members of LulzSec who had launched the attacks against Mastercard and Paypal. During this time, security researcher Aaron Barr, CEO of HBGary Federal, was privately investigating the matter and claimed that he had identified the members who had performed the attacks, and had proof of the matter. Aaron Barr's emails on the matter were leaked to the Internet and may be found on a number of websites.[18] According to the leaked emails, Barr used Internet Relay Chat (public channel) to obtain the handle names of those members involved in the attack. He then used social media such as Facebook and LinkedIn to allegedly look at friends and family of the hacker group. He then made inferences to the point where he claimed he had identified members who launched the attack. Members of LulzSec retaliated claiming he had put many innocent individuals in danger. If Barr had indeed used social media to retrieve this information, his methodology remains unclear. Most people are unable to view one's Facebook account unless they befriend them. There are, however, methods to hack into a Facebook account without authorisation.[19] It is likely that Barr had indeed accessed this information without authorisation. Members of LulzSec responded to Barr's claims by allegedly copying 40,000 emails and making it available on piratebay, launching a denial of service attack to his company's website, and posting the message, "now the Anonymous hand is bitch-slapping you in the face".

According to the UK newspaper The Guardian, the exposed emails from HBGary revealed that they, along with security firms Palantir and Berico, "were discovered to have conspired to hire out their information war capabilities to corporations which hoped to strike back at perceived enemies, including US activist groups, WikiLeaks and journalist Glenn Greenwald."[20] An interview with Dreyfus revealed a similar theme of corporations and governments engaging "cowboy security firms" to perform attacks either directly on hacktivism websites and other targets. Dreyfus also revealed that there were several recent attacks performed by cowboy security firms who have made it look as though such attacks came from Anonymous. The contracting out of intelligence services, "for hire cyber-attack

---

[18] For example, the emails are provided on The Old Computer at http://www.theoldcomputer.co m/blog/index.php?start=60.

[19] AusCERT 2011 presentation.

[20] Huffington Post 2 October 2011.

services" by governments to security firms was also exposed in the Canadian television program The Agenda.[21]

Arrests of LulzSec members in the US and the UK has not had the effect of deterring hacktivism. Other members of the group have met the arrests with counter-attacks of law enforcement databases, and any organisation who they see as having aided in the arrest of these individuals. It is important to note that some companies such as Twitter have fought court orders to reveal account details and other information about their clients. The Twitter case against Wikileaks members may even be taken to the Supreme Court of the United States.

Members of LulzSec and Anonymous have been arrested in the UK and the US, charges pending, and outcomes unknown at this time.

Nineteen year old Ryan Cleary was arrested in Essex in the United Kingdom and has been charged under the Computer Misuse Act for his hacking effort of the UK's Serious Organised Crime Agency. He is also alleged to have broken into many other law enforcement agencies both in the United Kingdom and the United States. Cleary is said to be a member of LulzSec.

Arizona college student Cody Kretsinger, alleged member of LulzSec, was arrested and charged with multiple counts of conspiracy and unauthorised impairment of a protected computer in the United States for allegedly hacking Sony Pictures Entertainment. The hacking is said to be that of Sony's computer system, which was compromised in May and June in 2011. LulzSec, unlike Anonymous, performs hacks both for political reasons and "just for fun" or "just for laughs" (lulz is computer slang for laughs). LulzSec has not formally announced any political reason for the Sony hack. Interesting, however, are the many media comments and blog responses that sympathised with LulzSec and find the lapse security measures of such corporations to be the worst offender. As one blogger writes:

> The main offender here is Sony. They were fully aware of the vulnerability of their current system. They were just too lazy to fix it. All it took was a Google search and some script kiddies entered in one SQL line and broke into the system. This wasn't a "zero day attack", it was a well known vulnerability to their system that was public. It's like having a stack of money just behind a gate with no lock. All it takes is one simple well known action and you are in. Why do you think class action lawsuits were charged against Sony if it wasn't their fault?[22]

Other members of LulzSec have been arrested and detained in Italy, Switzerland, and the United States for computer offences for hacking a number of different websites. It is much more difficult to see any public benefit or ethical conduct in many of LulzSec's operations, other than the media coverage exposing the poor security habits of most corporations and governments. Security experts have been urging companies and governments to improve their outdated and insecure protection of their systems for decades. During the last decade, however, many corporations still don't use basic encryption to protect personal information of their customers, nor do they adequately protect their own assets.

---

[21] The Agenda, 25 October 2011.

[22] [8].

2.1.2 Self-Disclosure

Self-disclosure is when the vendor/owner of a product voluntarily discloses a security vulnerability of its product. In some instances the disclosure is performed in spite of the fact that there is no legal obligation to do so. In other instances the law requires disclosure in order to be compliant with existing regulations.

2.1.2.1 Organisation Voluntarily Releases Information on Security Vulnerability

Some organisations have voluntarily released information about security vulnerabilities. In some instances the incident may have been reported in the media based on the voluntary release of the vulnerability and breach of personalised data. In other incidents, the shareholders and affected individuals may be notified. On the one hand, it could be seen that such voluntary disclosure would attract negative attention, especially with the aftermath of related media stories. On the other hand, organisations might be more inclined to be seen as ethical in the eyes of their customers by actively reporting on disclosures and letting customers know that they are taking the matter seriously.

Case Study: Telstra

Telstra is the largest Internet Service Provider in Australia. In late 2011 a member from the broadband community going by the name of Whirlpool (unclear if this is the same member of LulzSec) discovered that an Internet search page exposed millions of customer details including usernames, passwords, and account numbers.[23] Telstra immediately removed the site and began investigating the security vulnerability that led to this massive data breach. Under Australian law, companies are not compelled to notify their customers when their personal information has been breached. Data breach notification laws will be addressed in Chap. 5.

2.1.2.2 Disclosure as Compliance

In some situations an organisation may be compelled under regulations to disclose information about computer security including vulnerabilities. This requirement is usually in response to a security incident such as the leaking of personal files. While there are a number of incidents to consider, the excellent reporting and investigation of the Hong Kong leakage of confidential information related to corrupt police, and the Choice Point data breach incident in the United States.

---

[23] [9].

Case Study: Hong Kong Independent Police Complaints Council

On Friday, March 10, the South Morning china Post reported that 20,000 complaint files against the Hong Kong police were freely accessible on the Internet on the website www.china2easy.com. Included in the complaint files were the names, addresses, and identification numbers of complainants, the dates of the complaints, and in a few instances, details of previous criminal convictions. Some of the more serious cases involved corruption, fraud, and sexual abuse. While the information on the website was quickly removed, the information could still be accessed several days later via the Google Archives and Cache. It soon became apparent that this information had somehow been leaked and made available on the Internet some three years earlier, although it was discovered much later by shareholder activist David Webb.[24]

Several individuals from the complaint files lodged complaints with the Hong Kong Privacy Commissioner. The Privacy Commissioner launched a full and public investigation of the incident. The facts of the ICPP incident were not at the time conclusive but seemed to indicate that human oversight was responsible. At the time of the investigation the exact types of technologies and security measures were not disclosed to the public. Under a direct order from the Office of the Privacy Commissioner, all parties involved with the incident were forced to disclose all aspects of the incident including all known vulnerabilities, security policies, outsourcing documents and all aspects of this disturbing disclosure of personal information.[25]

Case Study: Choice Point

Two major data breaches of US companies Choice Point and TJ Max garnered international media scrutiny and attracted a litany of legal attention. In 2005 it was discovered that there had been a major breach of Choice Points data systems. Under California data breach notification law, Choice Point was obliged to send out 35,000 California residents notices that their personal information had been breached for fraudulent identity theft purposes. Originally notification was only to California residents but then later expanded to include notification to affected customers in various other states. Overall, the ChoicePoint data breach affected over 150,000 individuals. ChoicePoint notified the affected individuals as well as the FTC. The FTC filed suit against ChoicePoint where the organisation paid a $10 million dollar fine and was ordered to set aside $5 million for restitution. After only 131 individuals came forth with monetary claims, the FTC refunded only $141, 753 and returned the remainder of the fund to ChoicePoint.[26] The U.S. Government

---

[24] [10].

[25] [11].

[26] [12].

Accountability Office studied 24 publicly reported breaches and similarly found the compromised data from only three breaches was used illegally afterwards such as fraud. Data breach notification laws will be examined in Chap. 5.

References

1. Pfleeger C, Pfleeger S (2006) Security in Computing, 4th edn. Prentice Hall, Englewood Cliffs
2. Moses A (2011) Super bad: first State set Police on Man who Showed Them How 770,000 accounts could be ripped off. The Sydney Morning Herald available at http://www.smh.com.au/it-pro/security-it/super-bad-first-state-set-police-on-man-who-showed-them-how--770000-accounts-could-be-ripped-off-20111018-1lvx1.html
3. Zenz K (2008) Cyber Crime within the Russian Federation (presentation at AusCERT)
4. Greenberg A (2012) Shopping for Zero-Days: a price list for Hackers' secret software exploits. Forbes http://www.forbes.com/sites/andygreenberg/2012/03/23/shopping-for-zero-days-an-price-list-for-hackers-secret-software-exploits/
5. Greenberg A (2012) Meet the Hackers who sell spies the tools to crack your PC (and get paid six-figure fees). Forbes http://www.forbes.com/sites/andygreenberg/2012/03/21/meet-the-hackers-who-sell-spies-the-tools-to-crack-your-pc-and-get-paid-six-figure-fees/2/
6. Watts S (2010) Newsnight Online 'Chat' with Lulz Security Hacking Group. http://www.bbc.co.uk/news/technology-13912836
7. Leyden J (2010) Anonymous attacks PayPal in 'Operation Avenge Assange' (6 Dec 2010, 20 July 2011). The Register available at http://www.theregister.co.uk/2010/12/06/anonymous_launches_pro_wikileaks_campaign/
8. Risling G (2011) Cody Kretsinger: Arizona College Student, Charged in Sony Hacking Case (Sept 22). Huffington Post at http://www.huffingtonpost.com/2011/09/23/cody-kretsinger-arizona-c_n_977490.html
9. Colley A (2011) Telstra investigated over Data Breach. The Australian (Dec 9) http://www.theaustralian.com.au/australian-it/telstra-investigated-over-data-breach/story-e6frgakx-1226218501826
10. Maurushat A (2006) Who let the Cat our of the Bag. Part 1 Hong Kong Law J 36
11. Privacy Commissioner (2006) Releases the IPCC releases the Investigation Report. http://www.pcpd.org.hk/english/infocentre/press_20061026b.html
12. Cate F (2009) Information security breaches: looking back and thinking ahead. The Centre for Information Policy Leadership (2008) available at www.informationpolicycentre.com/ (last accessed Oct 22)

Chapter 3
Discovery and Dissemination of Discovering Security Vulnerabilities

Abstract The method of discovering security vulnerabilities raises separate legal and ethical issues apart from the disclosure of such vulnerabilities. This chapter explains the various methods of discovering and disseminating vulnerabilities (such as the use of a honeynet, youtube concept of proof videos, zero day exploit markets) and provides for an explanation of each method, then uses a case study where possible to introduce legal and ethical issues.

3.1 Introduction

While there are many methods discovering, and disseminating security vulnerabilities, some methods expose the discloser to legal liability as well as to criminal charges. The different methods of discovering and disseminating vulnerabilities are identified in this chapter. Possible legal liability and criminal provisions are identified against each method but not fully explored until subsequent chapters.

Many methods of discovery and dissemination involve intelligence gathering. The most common methods are traffic observation traffic (on IRC channels, or in other protocols such as HTTP, on P2P networks), honeynets, reverse engineering and collection of information in hacker forums and chatrooms.

3.2 Discovery: Honeynets and Traffic Observation

Much intelligence gathering is performed using honeynets. Honeynets are information gathering places where an entity deliberately allows the computer to become infected. As described by two of the most authoritative experts, Neilss Provos and Thorsten Holz, "a honeynet is a closely monitored computing resource that we want to be probed, attacked, or compromised". More precisely, a honeypot is "an information system resource whose value lies in unauthorized or illicit use of that resource."[1] Security vendors, researchers, Internet Service Providers, banks and

---

[1] [1].

many other organisations often use virtual honeynets to gather information about how malware is being used. In doing so, information is collected as to how the computer becomes compromised, what types of malware are installed, and it allows the researcher to observe the computer code to ascertain the nature of how, for example, a particular software works. If the software is encrypted, then the operator of the honeynet may need to decrypt the instructions. By discovering methods of attack and malware dissemination, the researcher can also discover the vulnerabilities that allowed such attacks. The data and/or executable code may be encrypted on arrival, but it has to be decrypted before use. It is therefore accessible to the investigator in the computer's main memory, through the use of a debugging tool that enables programs to be run step-by-step and memory inspected at each step.

By identifying how malware behaves, and how it spreads may also help to identify the particular vulnerability that was exploited to enable the malware in the first place. Honeynets are typically used to identify and develop specific intelligence for malware. Like most technology, it is a double edged sword. It is also possible to use a honeynet to see how legitimate software reacts in various instances, and to examine malware exploits vulnerabilities in software, hardware and operating systems.

This information benefits security vendors by allowing them to develop better anti-virus and anti-spyware software. The information is equally valuable to corporations and organisations in providing information about vulnerabilities in their network. Internet service providers use the information to develop spam filters, to identify vulnerable points in their networks, to identify customers at risk and so forth. The use of honeynets has attracted attention in the United States where there has been an ongoing debate about ethical and legal issues surrounding the use of honeynets. Many of the ethical and legal issues are intertwined with the use of honeynets. There are potential problems with unauthorised access, as well as issues such as entrapment and interception of communications. According to expert Richard Salgado, "The very purpose of your honeypot is to be attacked... so it's a little odd to say we're doing our monitoring of this computer to prevent it from being monitored."[2]

Security researchers are not exempt from either unauthorised data provisions, nor are they lawfully able to intercept communications as most communications, whether criminal or otherwise, are protected under the law. Honeynets intercept communications without permission. Some jurisdictions as will be seen in Chap. 4 allow for exemptions but these are few and are limited to very specific instances. The interception of communications in a honeynet is lawful where owners of compromised machines as well as the malware writers/owners are notified (Eg. via banner display) that their communications are being monitored. This, of

---

[2] Salgado, R., "The Legal Ramifications of Operating a Honeypot" (2005) IEEE Magazine Security and Privacy, vol. 1. Salgado is considered as a recognized authority of legal issues in honeypots. He is former attorney with the United States Department of Justice, Computer Crime and Intellectual Property Section, U.S. Department of Justice, and Senior Counsel with Yahoo!, Inc. He is now Senior Counsel of Google and Adjunct Professor at Stanford University.

course, would defeat the purpose of a honeynet. The other way to legally operate a honeynet is to establish a production machine, wait to first be attacked, then use the honeynet. The malicious traffic is rerouted to the honeynet only after an attack on the production server is initiated. In this instance the situation is similar to self-defense to protect property.

The case study of the Torpig botnet is useful in exploring some of the issues with discovery methods, then analysing and using traffic data, whether it be through a honeynet, sinkhole or similar intelligence gathering techniques. While Torpig is not directly related to security disclosure, the methods involved in intelligence gathering whether it be for malware, botnets, vulnerabilities or other computer security aspects illustrated in Torpig are similar in nature, and identical in terms of potential legal consequences.

First, a botnet is a collection of remotely controlled and compromised computers that are controlled by a bot master/botherder. Botnets utilise a series of technologies, software programs, and methods. As part of a botnet's operations, malware may be installed onto the compromised computers. A botnet receives its instructions in the form of a computer software program known as a 'bot'. Many bots may be categorised as malware.

The Torpig botnet appears to have originated in Eastern Europe in 2005. In 2009, a group of university researchers at the University of California, Santa Barbara (UCSB) infiltrated the Torpig botnet to gather intelligence as to the botnets inner workings.[3] They used a virtual honeypot[4] to record the commands the bot receives, monitor the malicious activities, and determine which computers had been compromised. The aim of the researchers was not to take the botnet down, but to merely gather intelligence on the botnet and share this information with law enforcement, CERTs, and other security researchers.

The UCSB research team was able to take over the C&C source of the Torpig botnet for 10 days. During this time they discovered that there were two C&C methods through a reverse engineering of the domain generation algorithm. The first C&C used encrypted HTTP protocol linking to domain names. The bot was not detected by any anti-virus or anti-spyware programs. The backup C&C was located in a separate botnet known as Mebroot. Mebroot was obscured from view by means of a rootkit. The domain name C&C generated a weekly domain name, thereby moving the C&C to a new location each week. When the C&C was not functioning properly by rotating through a fast-flux each week, Torpig then began to generate a new C&C every day, and if every day did not work, the botnet switched C&C through a rapid fast-flux of every 20 min.[5]

The UCSB team recorded 180,000 unique hosts making up the botnet. During the 10 days, they observed messages flowing from the bots back to the botnet master containing banking details from over 8,310 accounts in 410 financial

---

[3] [2].

[4] "A honeynet is a closely monitored computing resource that we want to be probed, attacked, or compromised" Provos, see footnote 1.

[5] [3].

institutions, together with 1,660 sets of credit card details. The researchers describe how the banking information was obtained as follows:

> Torpig uses phishing attacks to actively elicit additional, sensitive information from its victims, which, otherwise, may not be observed during the passive monitoring it normally performs. These attacks occur in two steps. First, whenever the infected machine visits one of the domains specified in the configuration file (typically, a banking web site), Torpig issues a request to an injection server. The server's response specifies a page on the target domain where the attack should be triggered (we call this page the trigger page, and it is typically set to the login page of a site), a URL on the injection server that contains the phishing content (the injection URL), and a number of parameters that are used to fine tune the attack (e.g., whether the attack is active and the maximum number of times it can be launched). The second step occurs when the user visits the trigger page. At that time, Torpig requests the injection URL from the injection server and injects the returned content into the user's browser. This content typically consists of an HTML form that asks the user for sensitive information, for example, credit card numbers and social security numbers. These phishing attacks are very difficult to detect, even for attentive users. In fact, the injected content carefully reproduces the style and look-and-feel of the target web site. Furthermore, the injection mechanism defies all phishing indicators included in modern browsers. For example, the SSL configuration appears correct, and so does the URL displayed in the address bar. An example screen-shot of a Torpig phishing page for Wells Fargo Bank is shown in Fig. 2. Notice that the URL correctly point to https://online.wellsfargo.com/signon, the SSL certificate has been validated, and the address bar displays a padlock. Also, the page has the same style as the original web site.[6]

The researchers recorded the phishing scams noting that 14 % related to jobs/resumes, 7 % were money making proposals, 6 % sports fans, 5 % exams and websites on worrying about grades, and 4 % were related to sex.[7] The researchers reported that the banking information collected was sold to multiple parties in the underground economy. Symantec also followed the Torpig botnet, noting that credit card details were fetching a rate between $10 and $25, while bank accounts were worth between $10 and $100, with total profit estimates from anywhere of $830,000–$8.3 million.[8] It is reasonable to infer that Torpig's botnet master(s) were motivated by financial gain.

The researchers expressed concern at the risk of being pursued by law enforcement as well as potential retribution victims. They have openly expressed a strong belief that the Torpig botnet originated in Eastern Europe and may be linked to organised criminal groups.[9] The researchers contacted the FBI during the timeframe within which the researchers had infiltrated the botnet. Once notified, the FBI sent the data to the National Cyber-Forensics and Training Alliance, a not-for-profit security corporation.[10] The FBI made requests to registrars to de-register the domain names of the documented C&Cs. The researchers note that on the day that the FBI was notified, the C&C migrated from domain names to the

---

[6] Kemmerer, see footnote 3.

[7] See footnote 3.

[8] [4].

[9] See footnote 3.

[10] *See* Poulsen, footnote 13 in Chap. 1.

encrypted rootkit known as Mebroot. As the researchers note, this is likely not a coincidence.[11] The Mebroot botnet is encrypted. No researcher at the time was able to crack Mebroot's encryption.

Some of this information was shared with the FBI. Researchers not only identified compromised computers but they peered into email contents from infected machines to see how the Torpig botnet was spreading. They found out exactly what email messages and websites were behind the spread of the botnet including fake anti-virus software websites. In doing so, they broke many laws including unauthorised access, privacy breaches and trespass. At one point in the Torpig presentation the researcher indicated that when the FBI was informed of what the researchers had done, they responded with the likes of, "We've been trying rather unsuccessfully to get approval to do this type of investigation for a long time." This presents us with two significant problems. First, law enforcement is unable to perform the type of investigation necessary to combat security threats due to legal safeguards. For example, it is not feasible to obtain (much less do so at the speed of a mutating botnet!), a thousand third party warrants to examine the contents of bot owners computers to see how a botnet is replicating. Second, the operation of a virtual honeynet as seen in the cases of the Torpig botnet, involved breaking the law by unauthorised act, interception of communications, invading privacy, and trespass. As will be seen in Chap. 4, there are no security exemptions found in the legislation for unauthorised access, modification or interference of data or data systems.

3.3 Discovery: Reverse Engineering

Reverse engineering is the study of a finished object or software, and its behaviour, to determine how it works. This may include the observation of the code while it is running to learn the behaviour of the software when processing different input. In a non-computer context this could be the equivalent of taking apart a car's motor, studying it then putting it back together to see how it is made up, and driving it in order to find out how it works. In a computer context, reverse engineering refers to the examination of the available code, and exercise of it, to determine how the software works. Reverse engineering can be categorised as passive and active. Passive reverse engineering involves the mere examination of source code. Many programs, however, do not display the source code of the product making passive reverse engineering impossible. Where the source code is not available or where it is encrypted, active reverse engineering techniques are required.

A common active reverse engineering technique uses auditing of binary code often done through decompilation or disassembly.[12] Decompilation is the process of taking executable code and turning it into high level language source code such

---

[11] See footnote 3.

[12] [5].

as Java. Disassembly is similar to decompilation only it involves turning executable code into assembly language. Assembly language is not as easy to analyse as high level language source code, but the conversion process is far more reliable. In advanced reverse engineering, techniques such as debugging, fuzzing, proxies and decryption are used.[13] Active reverse engineering techniques involve the use of specific software tools to perform reverse engineering; they cannot be performed through the naked eye observing source code. Advanced reverse engineering techniques, especially when used to decrypt ciphertext,[14] may require significant time, effort and large quantities of data. While encrypted algorithms may be decrypted with a public key, decryption without the key remains difficult and, in some cases, not possible to decrypt.[15]

Where reverse engineering is successful it may help to identify possible vulnerabilities of a computer program.

3.4 Dissemination: Hacking Forums, Mailing Lists and Blogs

Information gathering may also be done by observing hacking forums and chatrooms. There are many chatrooms, carder forums and blogs that openly discuss exploits, how to set up botnets, where to acquire stolen credit card numbers, the selling of stolen identity documents and credit card numbers, and other matters related to cybercrime.[16]

Hacking chatrooms, mailing lists, blogs and websites have been common since the 1990s when the Internet starting to become better known. The full disclosure movement spawned a number of chatrooms, blogs, websites and mailing lists. One of the first was a mailing list known as Bugtraq. Bugtraq commenced as a mailing list of full disclosures of security bugs. Its unique feature was that the preferred course of action to first notify the software company of its vulnerability to allow the company to patch it before disclosure. Bugtraq published all full disclosures, regardless if they remained unpatched. Today, the mailing list is hosted by Security Focus community (http://www.securityfocus.com/) and remains committed to the principle that the security community needed a place to come together and share its collected wisdom and knowledge. According to the website

---

[13] Poulsen, footnote 13 in Chap. 1, pages 336–358.

[14] Ciphertext is data that has been encrypted. The goal of decryption is to convert the ciphertext to plaintext which can then be understood. *See generally* Anderson, R., *Security Engineering: A Guide to Building Dependable Distributed Systems 2nd ed* (Wiley 2008) Chapters 5 Cryptography and 6 Distributed Systems for excellent discussion on cryptography, encryption and decryption, pages 129–213.

[15] Anderson, above.

[16] Poulsen, footnote 13 in Chap. 1.

as verified and confirmed in computer security books, Security Focus offers three leadings disclosure and sharing databases:

- BugTraq is a high volume, full disclosure mailing list for the detailed discussion and announcement of computer security vulnerabilities. BugTraq serves as the cornerstone of the Internet-wide security community.
- The SecurityFocus Vulnerability Database provides security professionals with the most up-to-date information on vulnerabilities for all platforms and services.
- SecurityFocus Mailing Lists allow members of the security community from around the world to discuss all manner of security issues. There are currently 31 mailing lists; most are moderated to keep posts on-topic and to eliminate spam.[17]

Another similar disclosure website is VX Heavens which acted as an archive of malware, security vulnerabilities and library of papers from multiple disciplines related to computer security, malware and hacking in general. VX Heavens, unlike Bugtraq, has attracted legal scrutiny over the years. My own paper written with Professor John Aycock was uploaded to VX Heavens without authorisation. This isn't abnormal in that many people link and upload material found on the Internet. The paper at question, however, was not freely available on the Internet but was at the time only available to those members of VirusBulletin. Nonetheless, I always felt that it was an honour to have any of my material on the website.

VX Heavens website operated out of the Ukraine. The Ukrainian police reportedly raided the spot where the operators were located, and had the website shut down in the name of combating cybercrime.[18] VX Heavens website has appeared in mirrored sites such as http://vx.netlux.org/index.html. A message from the front page of the site (written in both Ukrainian and English) states

> Viruses don't harm, ignorance does!…
>
> For many years we were tried hard to establish a reliable work of the site, which supplied you with a professional quality information on systems security and computer virology. We do always believe that a true research in any field (computer virology included) is only possible in the atmosphere of trust, openness and mutual assistance.
>
> Unfortunately…
>
> Friday, 23 March, the server has being seized by the police forces due to the criminal investigation (article 361-1 Criminal Code of Ukraine—the creation of the malicious programs with an intent to sell or spread them) based on someone's tip-off on "placement into the free access malicious software designed for the unauthorized breaking into computers, automated systems, computer networks".
>
> The absurdity of such statement we need to prove in the court…
>
> We are sorry, but until the case is still open we are unable to offer our services in any form.[19]

This particular case against VX Heavens is compelling for three reasons. Firstly, the takedown of the website occurred in a supposed "cybercrime safe haven"; the

---

[17] Security Focus at http://securityfocus.com.

[18] [6].

[19] Available at http://vx.netlux.org/index.html.

Ukraine has been a jurisdiction with a high rate of cybercrime and a poor record of taking an active response to the problem. Secondly, VX Heavens is seen in the industry as "old-school" and is not seen as being linked with organised cybercrime but rather as a hobbyist website. This *may* indicate that the raid was a mere political jest to say to the international community, "look, we're policing cybercrime." Third, it is a clear signal that publishing security vulnerabilities and publishing malware regardless of whether you commit a criminal offence such as fraud with this knowledge, will attract criminal sanction, at least in the Ukraine. It is difficult to see on the face of this charge how the Ukrainian government will prove that the website authors actually created malware as opposed to the mere publication of malware.

3.5 Dissemination: YouTube Proof of Concept Video for Zero Day Exploit

Many security experts and hackers have begun to post "proof of concept videos" that demonstrate, in part or in full, a security vulnerability in a product and how to exploit it. Proof of concept videos act as a vehicle to proving that you have indeed discovered and possibly exploited a bug, as opposed to merely claiming without proof that you have discovered a bug. The proof of concept may expose a security vulnerability or it may demonstrate how to exploit a vulnerability.

3.5.1 Case Study: An Unidentified Security Researcher's Proof of Concept Video for Zero day Exploit

I occasionally received communication from members of the security research community asking the legal questions in relation to security work. The following example states the communication between myself and a security researcher who, in spite having given me permission to publish his situation, shall remain anonymous and unidentifiable. The person writes:

> You probably have heard about the cyber attacks on Google, Adobe, and other high-profile companies. The attackers used an exploit to target a previously unknown vulnerability in Internet Explorer. The exploit used in the attack went public so both HD Moore (from the Metasploit project) and myself released separately proof-of-concept exploits to take advantage of the vulnerability in Internet Explorer. To my knowledge, during that time there were only 3 public exploits that targeted the vulnerability. The original exploit that was uploaded to Wepawet on January 14th, HD Moore's exploit that was added to Metasploit on January 15th, and my exploit that was posted on my website on January 17th. Both the original exploit and the one in Metasploit have reliability issues, which I improved in my version of the exploit. I've noticed recently that McAfee have posted videos on YouTube that use my proof-of-concept exploit without my permission to promote one of their products. I've also noticed that McAfee have added my website to their "Pornography" category after a McAfee customer mentioned on their blog that several

of their products failed to prevent my exploit from working. Please note that my website has never been associated with any form of pornographic content. People in the United Arab Emirates (UAE) and Saudi Arabia have mentioned to me that my website has been blocked in their countries. After doing some research, I found out that both the UAE and Saudi Arabia use a McAfee product (McAfee SmartFilter) to censor web content. I contacted McAfee and I told them that I believe they intentionally added my website to the pornography category after someone pointed out the flaws in their products to prevent people who use their filtering product from accessing my website and damage my reputation. I also told that if my website is not removed from their database and I don't get a official response about the issue, I will contact the press and file a lawsuit against them. I quickly received a response from the Vice President for Threat Research who simply mentioned that they reviewed my website and changed its category to "Technical Information".

Please note that my website is still blocked in the UAE, Saudi Arabia, and other countries that rely on McAfee SmartFilter to censor web content.

A number of legal issues are represented in this scenario which will briefly be summarised below and later expanded on in Chap. 5 which addresses copyright and defamation. Below represents the information I sent in response to the initial request for information. As such, the following sections read more like a communication.

Whether or not there is a copyright infringement for the proof of concept video depends on a number of things including: (1) permission to use (implied or explicit)—if the entity had obtained the information from your website and you have no terms and conditions about your work on your website, it is debateable at law whether they can copy and use it; (2) how much of the proof of concept that was utilized is also an issue as there is a fair dealing/fair use right for unsubstantial proportions of a work protected by copyright, (3) attribution to you, no matter if a little or a lot was used, is required under the law. All of this to say, that the above analysis depends on whether McAfee used your proof of concept or the proof of concept from HD Moore and Metasploit. This is crucial as the Metasploit site uses a BSD licence. The relevant terms are listed below:

Redistribution and use in source and binary forms, with or without modification, are permitted provided that the following conditions are met:
* Redistributions of source code must retain the above copyright notice, this list of conditions and the following disclaimer.
* Redistributions in binary form must reproduce the above copyright notice, this list of conditions and the following disclaimer in the documentation and/or other materials provided with the distribution.
* Neither the name of Rapid7 LLC nor the names of its contributors may be used to endorse or promote products derived from this software without specific prior written permission.
THIS SOFTWARE IS PROVIDED BY THE COPYRIGHT HOLDERS AND CONTRIBUTORS "AS IS" AND ANY EXPRESS OR IMPLIED WARRANTIES, INCLUDING, BUT NOT LIMITED TO, THE IMPLIED WARRANTIES OF MERCHANTABILITY AND FITNESS FOR A PARTICULAR PURPOSE ARE DISCLAIMED. IN NO EVENT SHALL THE COPYRIGHT OWNER OR CONTRIBUTORS BE LIABLE FOR ANY DIRECT, INDIRECT, INCIDENTAL, SPECIAL, EXEMPLARY, OR CONSEQUENTIAL DAMAGES (INCLUDING, BUT NOT LIMITED TO, PROCUREMENT OF SUBSTITUTE GOODS OR SERVICES; LOSS OF USE, DATA, OR PROFITS; OR BUSINESS INTERRUPTION) HOWEVER CAUSED AND ON ANY THEORY OF LIABILITY, WHETHER IN CONTRACT,

STRICT LIABILITY, OR TORT (INCLUDING NEGLIGENCE OR OTHERWISE) ARISING IN ANY WAY OUT OF THE USE OF THIS SOFTWARE, EVEN IF ADVISED OF THE POSSIBILITY OF SUCH DAMAGE.[20]

The BSD License allows a company like McAfee or anyone else to use the source code, even for commercial purposes, providing the use meets the licensing terms. More information about copyright issues is explored in Chap. 5.

The listing of your website or part of your website that demonstrates your exploit as pornography doesn't have a legal solution. It is next to impossible to prove that McAfee added your site to their 'pornography' list due its nature as showing a vulnerability in their product. It is possible and even likely that a mistake was made. That being said, describing an exploit in theory would have nothing to do with pornography. But as you have noted, they have removed your site from their pornography determination.

I'm not sure based on the enquiry whether there is a legal issue on censorship in Saudi Arabia (SA) or whether there are any practical ramifications from being categorised as "technical information". According to the information you have sent, you mention Saudi Arabia utilised McAfee SmartFilter but you would also know that they utilise a number of other technologies for Internet censorship purposes.[21] Proving that your site is blocked in SA due to a deliberate McAfee placement as banned content would be extremely difficult. I do not have sufficient knowledge about Saudi Arabian law to provide information to you. I am merely aware that this country filters a great deal of Internet content. On face value, there would be nothing illegal about filtering information that relates to exploits, even when that information comes from white hat researchers such as yourself. As you are aware, publishing exploits is a contentious topic with no clear legality on point. In fact, it is possible that publishing exploits where the code is later used to perform actual attacks can be construed under the law as "aiding and abetting" crime (to be examined in Chap. 4). This is not a stable area of law.

As to the blocked listing having damaged your reputation, I have never heard of a case where classification of a website as 'pornography' or illicit was found to constitute a defamatory statement (to be examined in Chap. 5). If you could get beyond this first hurdle, you would have to prove that your reputation was diminished in the eyes of your peers.

3.6 Dissemination: Public Conferences

There are many renowned computer security and hacking conferences such as BlackHat, DefCon, HackintheBox, and Chaos Communications Congress. These conferences are unique in that they bring together hackers, crackers (for criminal

---

[20] Metasploit Framework License Agreement available at http://www.metasploit.com/license.jsp.
[21] [7].

gain), white hat security researchers and experts, as well as law enforcement. Many of these conferences have hacking competitions where hackers earn money, reputation, and future clients for winning the competition by hacking the product and identifying security vulnerabilities. Typically the winner will accept the cash prize then hand over their method of exploiting the vulnerability over to the vendor. In this sense, the disclosure is limited to the vendor (and perhaps others present at the conference) and allows the vendor the opportunity to patch the vulnerability. Not all conference presentations where vulnerabilities are disclosed have the same happy ending, especially when the vendor has not elicited information about a vulnerability.

3.6.1 Case study: Blackhat Conference Where Cisco Router Vulnerability is Partially Disclosed

The most famous security vulnerability disclosure occurred during the 2005 Blackhat conference in Las Vegas where Michael Lynn gave a controversial presentation on vulnerabilities found in the Cisco router. You might say that this incident became the best case study for examining ethical and legal issues surrounding vulnerability disclosure.

Most of the Internet's infrastructure relies on Cisco's routers. Basically, routers are network devices that forward packets from one network to another. Security researchers have found flaws in Cisco's router software in the past but typically, such flaws were minor resulting only in a denial-of-service-attack. Michael Lynn, former security researcher with ISS, discovered what is believed to be the first known vulnerability of buffer overflow against a Cisco router. This significant vulnerability would allow an attacker to take over a network. The vulnerability has been described as a possible "Pearl Harbour" of vulnerabilities.[22]

Lynn's employer ISS was in discussion with Cisco about this vulnerability. Cisco was notified that ISS was to present on the router vulnerability at the 2005 Blackhat conference. Cisco's response was to threaten ISS with a lawsuit, and demand that the Blackhat organisers remove the presentation from the conference. At this point Cisco had neither fixed the vulnerability (though known to them) nor notified their clients of this potentially serious vulnerability.[23] No patch was, therefore, available at this time. Instead of backing down, Lynn quit ISS, told the Blackhat organisers that he would present on a different talk, then part way into his alternative presentation on VOIP, Lynn switched topics and began to discuss the serious flaw in Cisco's router. While Lynn did not publish his findings, and did not display the full vulnerability on screen, the partial descriptions and titbits of

---

[22] "Cisco, ISS file suit against rogue researcher Robert Lemos", SecurityFocus 2005-07-27 available at http://www.securityfocus.com/news/11259.

[23] Wired "Blackhat Interview with Michael Lynn" 2005.

code displayed allowed a room full of hackers to fully ascertain and share amongst themselves the shell code by the end of the presentation.[24]

Cisco filed law suits against Lynn and the Blackhat conference organisers claiming infringement of their intellectual property. As will be shown in Chap. 5, there is a research exemption and reverse engineering right under fair use doctrine, but any publication of the vulnerability may attract copyright sanctions. Copyright infringement can be filed both against the person who publishes (also oral presentation satisfies this requirement) as well as the distributors, in this case the conference organisers. The legal suits were dropped against Blackhat and Lynn on the condition that they restrain from future discussion about the vulnerability and the incident in general.

Code that exploits Cisco vulnerabilities often has a substantial market value. Experts have estimated that Lynn could have sold the vulnerability to Cisco at a market value of $250,000.[25]

3.7 Discovery and Dissemination: Internal and External Security Audits

Companies and organisations, both government and non-government, are subject to internal and external security audits in order to comply with applicable regulations. Regulations are often industry specific and vary from jurisdiction to jurisdiction. Audits are performed to address compliance with security standards and to report flaws where otherwise required by law. Both internal and external security audits may reveal security vulnerabilities in their networks. As security audits are performed by security researchers for a fee, the likeliness of these researchers then disclosing the vulnerabilities they have found is remote at best. Nonetheless, security audits remain a discovery method.

The greater issue remains how an organisation responds to the audit once vulnerabilities are identified. Failure to fix known security vulnerabilities provides incentive for third parties to disclose such security vulnerabilities with hopes of embarrassing the organisation.

References

1. Holz T, Provos N (2008) Virtual honeypots: from botnet tracking to intrusion detection (Addison-Wesley), p 8
2. Stone-Gross B, Cavallaro L, Gilbert B, Sydlowski M, Kemmerer R, Kruegel C, Vigna G (2009) Your botnet is my botnet: analysis of a botnet takeover CCS, ACM 978-1-60

---

[24] Discussion with computer security analyst who was present at the presentation.

[25] Wired, see footnote 23.

3. Kemmerer R (2010) "How to Steal a botnet and what can happen when you do" Google tech talk. Available at http://www.youtube.com/watch?v=2GdqoQJa6r4. Accessed 26 June 2010

4. Symantec, Report on the Underground Economy (2008) Available at http://www.symantec.com/content/en/us/about/media/pdfs/underground_Econ_Report.pdf. Accessed 28 June 2010

5. Harris S, Harper A, Eagle C, Ness J (2008) Gray hat hacking: the ethical hacker's handbook. McGraw Hill, pp 277–307

6. Cluley G (2012) VXHeavens old-school virus writing website, raided by police http://nakedsecurity.sophos.com/2012/03/28/vx-heavens-virus-writing-website-raided/

7. Maurushat A (2011) Australia. In: Cook S (ed) Freedom on the internet: a global assessment of internet and digital media. Freedom House, New York

Chapter 4
Criminal Offences: Unauthorised Access, Modification or Interference Comprovisions

Abstract Disclosure of security vulnerabilities attracts many different types of legal sanction. The most severe sanction is that of criminal law. This chapter identifies the main criminal offences that would apply to disclosure. The Convention on Cybercrime is briefly explained. The Convention is the only international agreement in the area, and virtually all Western democracies have adopted measures similar to those found in the Convention. The most important provision is what is known as "computer offences" which is often used interchangeably with "hacking offences." Australia will be used as a case study for the examination of "computer offences" along with more general criminal sanctions such as conspiracy, aiding and abetting/facilitation of a crime, and possession of hacking devices. Additionally, there is discussion around the importance of security research and public interest exemptions to computer offences. At present there are no exceptions to most forms of hacking and disclosure of security vulnerabilities. Elements of responsible disclosure are discussed at the end of the chapter. Tables are provided in Appendix A examining the provisions found in the Convention with the laws of certain jurisdictions including California and Federal US Law, Canada, Hong Kong, India, Japan and the UK.

4.1 Introduction

The most relevant legal framework for security disclosure involves what are known as "computer offences" or as they are also called, "hacking offences." Computer offences are part of the criminal framework. Computer offences consist of a suite of criminal provisions involving unauthorised access, modification and impairment/interference with data, data systems, computers, networks (a variety of terminology is used to connote computer). There is also a secondary suite of applicable criminal offences such as conspiracy and aiding and abetting in the commission of another crime. The first category of "computer offences" is criminalised under an international convention, and is criminalised in most first world, western democracies, and is increasingly criminalised in developing countries.

Most jurisdictions have enacted computer offenses which are often referred to as unauthorised access, modification or interference to data systems or electronic communications. For our purpose we will call them the "computer offenses."

Such criminal provisions generally address situations where any component of a computer (hard drive, software, network) is tampered with allowing for unauthorised access, modification, impairment or interference to data or a data system. Most criminal provisions distinguish mere access from modification and impairment/interference of data by looking at the intent and harm caused. The very nature of hacking, whether it be to expose security vulnerabilities or out of mere curiosity, involves the exploration (and sometimes exploitation) of vulnerabilities which, at a minimum, involve unauthorised access to data.

In the past, where a hacker has merely 'looked under the hood of a car without the owner's permission' but has not caused any harm, criminal charges have not been laid unless the hacker were peering into government systems or other systems linked to critical infrastructure such as the electrical grid or nuclear power plants. The law in many jurisdictions has been amended to cover a broad range of unauthorised access regardless of intent or harm caused including mere access to data by using someone else's username and password where it is unauthorised.[1]

The United States, Canada, European Union Members, and Australia (not an exhaustive list) have all enacted legislation that meets the requirements under the *Convention*. Comparative tables looking at California and Federal US Law, Canada, Hong Kong, India, Japan and the UK are found at the end of the book in Appendix A. Laws in these jurisdictions may contain slightly different wording but all contain similar provisions. As such I will write in generic terms for the types of relevant criminal provisions. These are:

- Computer Offenses (Unauthorised Access, Modification or Impairment/ Interference)
- Aiding and Abetting/Facilitation of a Crime
- Conspiracy
- Possession, Control or Supply of Data/Misuse of a Device
- The Laws of Misprision/Failure to Report a Serious Crime
- Security Exemption
- Public Interest Exemption
- Possible "Responsible Disclosure" Factors and Their Relation with the Law.

4.2 International Framework: Convention on Cybercrime

The *Convention on Cybercrime*, an agreement between member nations of the Council of Europe is the only enforceable international agreement in the area of cybercrime. It is somewhat unique in that it is open for signature by states who are not members of the Council of Europe. For example, the United States, Canada and Japan have all signed the *Convention* while other countries such as Australia have acceded to it.

---

[1] See for example, *The European Union passed the Framework Decision on Attacks Against the Information System 2005/222/JHA.*

The *Convention* has three key divisions: substantive law, procedural requirements and international cooperation. All signatories to the *Convention* must criminalise certain activities.[2]

The *Convention* creates four main categories of substantive offences:

1. offences against the confidentiality, integrity and availability of computer data and systems, comprising interference and misuse of devices;
2. computer-related offences such as forgery and computer fraud;
3. content-related offences, in particular the production, dissemination and possession of child pornography; and
4. offences related to infringement of copyright.

The most relevant category of crime to disclosure of security vulnerabilities is the first category (offences against computer data and systems) which I will refer to as "the computer offenses." These provisions, as will be discussed in the following section, potentially apply to the method of discovering security vulnerabilities such as honeynets, reverse engineering, hacking, proof of concept and so forth. The other categories, however, including fraud, child pornography and copyright are also potentially applicable to security disclosure where the vulnerability in question gives rise to fraud, possession or distribution of child pornography, or copyright infringement. The person responsible for publishing a known security vulnerability that is later used to exploit or install malware onto a system potentially becomes responsible for aiding and abetting in a crime, or conspiracy. In copyright, where the vulnerability of a copyright protection technology (referred to as technological protection measures) is revealed, both civil and criminal provisions of various copyright acts may apply (explored in Chap. 5).

The *Convention* also addresses the procedural aspects of cybercrime. The main categories here are:

1. expedited preservation of stored computer data;
2. expedited preservation and partial disclosure of traffic data;
3. production orders;
4. search and seizure of stored computer data;
5. real-time collection of traffic data; and
6. interception of content data.

Finally, the *Convention* contains provisions relating to international cooperation. While some of these provisions are contentious, the *Convention* allows a certain amount of flexibility how a nation might negotiate some of the issues. These may broadly be categorised as:

1. extradition;
2. mutual assistance; and
3. designation of a 24/7 network contact.

---

[2] This section of the monograph draws on work from [1].

Each of these international-cooperation components of the *Convention* exists to assist in categories of crimes under the *Convention,* but many jurisdictions such as Australia allow the cooperation and procedural aspects of the *Convention* to extend to any "serious offence."

4.3 Computer Offenses (Unauthorised Access, Modification or Impairment/Interference)

All jurisdictions compliant with the *Convention* make it illegal to access or modify data, or impair/interfere with electronic communications without authorisation. These are often referred to as computer offences. Computer offenses are typically classified as minor and serious. Unauthorised access for example will not attract the same severity of penalty that unauthorised impairment or interference would. I will use the jurisdiction of Australia to illustrate this point as my PhD in legal issues in computer security is based on the Cybercrime Convention and the law of Australia. As unauthorised access and modification (computer offenses) are criminalised in most Western democracies, and increasingly in developing countries as well, my use of Australia to illustrate points of law will be sufficient. Relevant cases from all jurisdictions, however, will be addressed.

Comparative Tables Found in Appendix A Demonstrate the Legal Position in California and Federal US Law, Canada, Hong Kong, India, Japan and the UK.

Computer offenses are outlined in Part 10.7 of the *Criminal Code 1995 (Cth)* of Australia. The CC is divided into serious computer offences which attract a penalty of up to 10 years imprisonment (Division 477.1 "Serious Computer Offences"), and other computer offences which attract a penalty of up to 2 years imprisonment (Division 477.2 "Unauthorised Modification of Data to Cause Impairment," Division 477.3 "Unauthorised Impairment of Electronic Communication," and Divisions 478 "Other Computer Offences").

Serious computer offences in s.477.1 require three elements to be met. First, a carriage service must be used in the commission of the offence (eg., the Internet). Second, the person must knowingly access, modify or impair data in an unauthorised manner. Accidental access or modification of data would not be caught under this provision. Third, there must be intent to commit a serious offence. "Serious offence" is defined in s.477.1(9) as "punishable by imprisonment for life or a period of 5 or more years." As the Model Code notes, "It is, essentially a specialised offence of attempt."[3] Obtaining credit card numbers with the intent to later use them in a fraudulent matter would be caught under s.480.4 which addresses dishonestly obtaining or dealing in personal financial information. This attracts a penalty of 5 years. Mere possession or control of financial information (eg., credit card numbers) through dishonest means where the information had *not* been used to commit a crime only attracts a penalty of 3 years (s.480.5). In the case of disclosure

---

[3] *Model Criminal Code*, Chapter 4 (January 2001), p. 104.

of a security vulnerability, merely publishing a vulnerability will not attract any of the "computer offenses." However, the later use of the vulnerability to access a database without authorisation, install malware onto a system, steal credit cards, or any other serious offence would be captured under these provisions. In the case of a fraudulent transfer of funds from a user's bank account to an unauthorised account, Divisions 134 and 135 which deal with fraud, would apply and attract a penalty in most instances ranging from 5 to 10 years. This activity would be a serious offence. Where banking details or credit card numbers are captured with an intent to use them in a fraudulent manner, s.477.1 is triggered. Section 477.1 offences attract a penalty that does not exceed the penalty of the serious offence [s.4.77.1(6)]. For example, if the fraudulent activity conducted by using a security vulnerability attracted 10 years of imprisonment, the court could not add 2 more years to the sentence for having modified data in an unauthorised manner. The facilitation of the commission of a serious offence through accessing, modifying or impairing data is also caught under s.477.1(4)(c). Where a hacker knowingly discloses a vulnerability to a group of people who he or she knows will take advantage of the vulnerability to steal financial could be construed as facilitation in the commission of a serious offence. As will be seen later, this could also be construed more generally as conspiracy to defraud or aiding and abetting in the commission of a crime.

Sections 477.2 ("unauthorised modification of data to cause impairment") and 477.3 ("unauthorised impairment to electronic communications") involve situations where there is no intent to commit a serious offence. Section 477.3, however, is aimed at the use of a denial of service attack. These sections differ from the "serious offence" provision in several ways. First, there is no need to demonstrate intent to commit a serious offence. The provisions apply to a person who knowingly or recklessly causes modification to data which, in turn, impairs access to, or the reliability, security or operation of a Commonwealth computer or electronic communication or uses a carriage service to do so. Impairment of data (s.477.2) or impairment of an electronic communication (s.477.3) is required for these provisions to apply. It is not helpful that "unauthorised access, modification or impairment" is defined in s.476.2 in a manner which merely repeats the use of the terms "modification" and "impairment" without defining these terms. The *Model Criminal Code* provides some assistance by explaining that the impairment to electronic communications provision is meant to apply to a denial of service attack.[4] Where a hacker uses an exploit to cause a data system to quit working or malfunction, the provision would apply. Where a security researcher merely posts a security vulnerability the provision would not apply. In this instance, the prosecution could use s.477.1(4)(d) where there is facilitation to commit a serious offence, or a more general provision of aiding and abetting a crime which will be explored later.

Most of these provisions could be considered, depending on the context, as offences that could apply to crimes committed using an exploit or disclosure of a security vulnerability. The first question to answer is whether there has been any

---

[4] MCC, above footnote 3.

form of *unauthorised* access, modification or impairment. The *Criminal Code* does not define what is meant by "unauthorised." There is no caselaw on what is meant by unauthorised access, modification or impairment of data in *this type of context*. The caselaw on unauthorised computer offences is dominated by unlawful employee access to databases while there is little caselaw where "hackers" or third parties were involved. For example, in *Johnston v Commissioner of Police*[5] addresses the misconduct of junior police officers accessing an information system without authorisation. In *Regan Gerard Gilmour v Director of Public Prosecutions (Commonwealth)*[6] an employee inserted data into a Commonwealth computer without authorisation. The decision of *Salter v DPP*[7] also involved unauthorised access of an employee to a police database. Justice Hulme referred to the 1993 decision of *Gilmour v Director of Public Prosecutions*[8] where Hayne J stated, "In the case of a hacker it will be clear that he has no authority to enter the system." *R v Stevens*[9] is one of the few publicly available decisions where an employee has not been involved. In this case the accused hacked into the ISP Ausnet, registered a fake account, and obtained credit card information of some of Ausnet's clients. Stevens made public his hack (including a few credit card numbers) to demonstrate the severe lack of security with Ausnet servers and forwarded the information to a journalist. He did not use the credit cards that he obtained; again, the purpose of the hack was to expose lackadaisical security practices. Some customers later complained that their credit cards were used abroad without authorisation. The decision does not, however, explore whether such credit cards were used abroad due to Steven's disclosure of the numbers or due to someone else having obtained such numbers as the result of Ausnet's insecure data storage practices.

There are hacking decisions in the United States, the United Kingdom, Canada, New Zealand, Australia and so forth but there are very few that address hacking for the purpose of disclosing vulnerabilities. These cases include criminal charges against hackers, both black and white hat, including David Nosal, Max Butler, David Ritz, Gary McKinnon, Ryan Cleary, Michael Lynn, Owen Walker, Jon Lech Johansen and Patrick Webster—to name but a few. The lack of prosecutions of those who disclose security vulnerabilities is not due to loopholes in the *Criminal Code* but is likely as the result of other factors. The first is political will to prosecute. As will be seen below, the case of Mangham is considered below highlighting the role of responsible disclosure in determining whether criminal charges are brought forward. Some of the generic challenges include: lack of police resources and training, traceback issues, digital forensics, volatility of evidence, and jurisdiction. Other reasons may include lack of political will to tackle

---

[5] (2007) NSWIR Comm 73.

[6] (1996) NSWSC 55.

[7] (2008) NSWSC 1325.

[8] (1995) 43 NSWLR 243.

[9] (1999) NSWCCA 69.

this area, especially when it is difficult to prove that the person who discloses the security vulnerability is the one who later commits a crime, and an underreporting of unauthorised incidents to police.

There is, however, one important decision regarding ethical hacking and security disclosure. *R v Mangham* is considered below. The New Zealand decision against Owen Walker is then considered as it provides a rich contrast to how courts may handle computer offenses.

4.3.1 Case Study: R. v Mangham

The only criminal law decision which clearly addresses the role of ethical hacking and security disclosure is the United Kingdom 2012 decision against Glenn Mangham. In *R v Mangham*[10] Glenn Mangham was charged with 3 counts of unauthorised access and modification of a computer but was convicted of 2 counts under the *1990 Computer Misuse Act*. He was sentenced initially to eight months imprison by the Southwark Crow Court. Later the Court of Appeal Criminal Division reduced the sentence from eight months to four months due to a lack of malicious intent.[11] Glenn Mangham, a university software developer student took advantage of a vulnerability to penetrate Facebook's firewall. Once inside, he continued to probe deeper in Facebook's network and at one point had downloaded a copy of Facebook's source code. Prosecutor Sandip Patel stated to the media that Mangham, "acted with determination, undoubted ingenuity and it was sophisticated, it was calculating," that he stole "invaluable" intellectual property and that the attack "represents the most extensive and grave incident of social media hacking to be brought before the British courts".[12] Mangham issued a lengthy public statement regarding the affair where he describes himself as an ethical hacker who had been awarded a fee previously for finding other security vulnerabilities within Yahoo![13] While Mangham takes responsibility for his actions in his statement, he makes a number of claims in which he feels should have been taken into account:

- He has routinely discovered security vulnerabilities of various organisations.
- Yahoo! had in the past paid him for his discovery of a vulnerability.
- He had made other discoveries of security vulnerabilities, reported them to the organisation in question then refused fees in the past.
- He mostly did not use anonymising software such as proxy servers as it was his intent to report any security vulnerabilities to Facebook.

---

[10] The decision was given in the Southwark Crow Court on 17/02/2012. The decision is not itself reported. Information was obtained through media stories. See BBC, "York Facebook hacking student Glenn Mangham jailed" 17 February, 2012.

[11] *Mangham R v,* Court of Appeal Criminal Division, EWCA 04/04/2012.

[12] [2].

[13] [3].

- He kept a copy of the valuable source code protected in a manner not connected to the Internet (or network connected to the Internet) which he points out as more securely stored Facebook's lack of protection.
- In the three weeks that he had a copy of the source code, he did not disclose it to any third parties, he did not make additional copies, and he did not take advantage of any of these vulnerabilities for illicit gain.
- Facebook now has a white hat bug bounty which allows security researchers to submit vulnerabilities through a formal channel. Mangham did not use this bug bounty as it did not exist at the time of this audit/incident in 2011.
- He claims that the figure of $200,000 of damages is unsubstantiated and likely to be exaggerated.

This case is potentially interesting for both ethical hackers and those who disclose security vulnerabilities on a number of grounds. The first is that most computer offense cases involve some form of malicious intent such as installing Trojans to illegally obtain information such as credit card numbers, or accessing customer databases of a competitor and so forth. Here there is a genuine claim of ethical hacking without somewhat indifferent intent. Certainly Mangham's intent was to obtain access to the source code without authorisation but there is no intent to use the source code to sell to a competitor (this would be worth millions of dollars) nor does there appear that he is interested in writing an exploit and then selling it back to Facebook as seen in the example of exploit market firms such as Vupen— the intent was later taken into account in reducing the sentence from eight to four months prison. My own interpretation of the decision is that he was prosecuted because he made a copy of one of the company's greatest assets, its source code. If he'd just been mucking about looking for vulnerabilities in the firewall, there may not have been any charges brought against him. Or if Mangham had just disclosed the vulnerability enabling him to get past Facebook's firewall it is doubtful that there would have been an investigation in the first place; he may have even been thanked and offered a fee. Further, if Mangham had used a recognised formal channel such as a bug bounty program there would likely have not been an investigation.

Factors involved in responsible disclosure are considered further in Sect. 4.9.

4.3.2 Case Study: R v Walker

The case of *R v. Walker* presents an interesting prospective on hacking. As the judge in the case highlights,

> Mr. Walker developed and used software that enabled him to remotely control infected computers. Collectively, the infected computers formed a robot network, commonly referred to as a bot net. Mr. Walker installed his bot code on tens of thousands of computers. He developed his code so that it could protect itself from discovery, spread automatically and identify and destroy rival bot codes. The code automatically disabled any antivirus software on an infected computer and prevented software from being updated, but in such a way that the computer owner believed the antivirus software he or she had

on his or her computer was still working and was successfully installing updates. Another bot code allowed Mr. Walker to operate through other computers as a proxy, making it harder for his activity to be traced back to him.[14]

Walker was brought up on several charges. The first charge was under s. 252(1) of the New Zealand *Crimes Act 1961* with accessing a computer system without authorization. The second charge related to interfering with a computer system under s. 250(2)(c) of the *Crimes Act 1961*. The third charge was the use of a computer system for dishonest purpose under s. 249(2)(a) of the *Crimes Act 1961*. Lastly, under s. 251(a) and (b) for possession of software for the purpose of committing a crime. Walker pleaded guilty to all charges. He could have been sentenced to up to 16 years of imprisonment under the four offences that he was charged with but was instead discharged without conviction, and was ordered to pay $9,526 NZD in reparation as well as to relinquish any assets acquired as a result of gains he achieved through use of his botnet.[15] The court noted that Walker committed the crimes over a two year period when he was aged 16–18. The court heard evidence of Walker's difficulty in socializing due to having Asperger's syndrome which is considered as part of the Autism Spectrum.

The judge looked at four factors when deciding how to sentence Owen Walker. First, what was the reason for the crime? The judge accepted that Walker's criminal behavior was motivated by curiosity and an intense interest in computers rather than motivated by criminal intent or malice.[16] The fact that he earned $36,174.64 from illegal activity did not seem to be a factor in the judge's decision. This particular finding is open to criticism. If a person were to break into a shopping mall, and replace all the store signs in the mall with substituted advertisements, one could easily conceive that a person may have done the act out of mischief and curiosity. However, if a person does the same act and is paid $36,174.64 by a third party to do so, the claim of mere curiosity becomes untenable. The judge's finding that there was no criminal intent in this case can be similarly be criticised as it signals to people that breaking and entering into a computer system will be treated lightly.

Second, the judge considered whether the harm was to individuals or a business enterprise. The judge noted that harm is difficult to assess in such cases because "it frequently cannot be identified."[17] Here he acknowledges that the only identifiable harm is the damage caused to the University of Pennsylvania website from a DDoS attack. The case does not state whether Walker performed a DDoS attack against the website or whether he rented his botnet out to someone for this purpose. The judge merely notes that $13,000 of damage was caused. It would not have been unreasonable for the court to estimate damages to those victim's machines which received unwanted adware courtesy of Walker's botnet. In this

---

[14] *R. v. Walker* HC HAM CRI2008-0750711 [2008] NZHC 1114 (15 July 2008), p. 4.

[15] Footnote 14 above, p. 37.

[16] Footnote 14 above, p. 37.

[17] Footnote 14 above, p. 24.

case, Walker installed the adware known as Dollar Revenue onto people's computers through his botnet.[18]

Arguably the facts in the Walker decision clearly point to sufficient intent to find Walker guilty of many accounts of unauthorised access and modification. The court, unlike in the Mangham decision, seems willing to accept that he was hacking out of curiosity and not out of any malicious intent regardless of the fact that he was financially profited from his hacking. Mangham did not profit from his hack. One cannot also think that the judge noted that Walker was a young man with Aspergers in the decision. Again, the most likely reason for the different outcome in Mangham as opposed to Walker is the action taken post access. Walker initiated a denial of service attack whereas Mangham copied the company's most highly valued intellectual property asset. Had Mangham merely launched a denial service attack, and found a few vulnerabilities in the firewall, he may have received a similar fate (no sentence).

4.4 Aiding and Abetting in the Commission of a Crime/Facilitation of a Crime

Both conspiracy and aiding and abetting are considered to fall within the doctrine of "law of extended common purpose liability" which is considered below. The doctrine considers under what circumstances and to what extent should those involved in a crime be held accountable in spite of the fact that they were not the actual person to commit the crime. For example, the driver of a car in an armed robbery or the person who held down the victim while another person raped or murdered the victim could be prosecuted under the extended common purpose liability.

The High Court of Australia has on several occasions considered the law of extended common purpose liability and has given specific scope to what is meant of s11.2 of the *CC* which makes it an offence to aid or abet the commission of a crime. The High Court of Australia in *Clayton v. R*[19] confirmed the decisions of *McAuliffe*[20] and *Gillard*[21] stating that, "If a party to a joint criminal enterprise foresees the possibility that another might be assaulted with intention to kill or cause really serious injury to that person, and despite that foresight, continues to participate in the venture, the criminal culpability lies in the continued participation in the join enterprise with the necessary foresight." The High Court of Australia places emphasis on continuing to play a role in a crime once it is foreseeable that a crime will be committed. *Clayton, McAuliffe* and *Gillard* were cases that all involved murders where the accused played a role in the murders such as drove the getaway vehicle but did not actually kill the victim.

---

[18] Walker likely installed adware other than DRsoftware onto user's systems.

[19] *Clayton v R* [2006] HCA 58.

[20] *McAuliffe v The Queen* [1995] 183 CLR 108.

[21] *Gillard v R* [2003] HCA 64.

In *Gillard* the accused stole and drove a van at the request of a man named Preston. Preston entered the van in disguise and had a gun. Preston had the accused phone a shop where the intended victim worked to see if he was indeed there. The accused drove Preston to the shop, watched Preston enter the shop, Preston then shot two men and injured another, and the accused drove Preston to another destination. After the incident the accused disposed of the van. The court found the accused guilty of murder by his complicit and continued cooperation with the accused due to the foreseeability that Preston would kill the individuals at the shop. The court stated that,

> The accused is held criminally responsible for his or her *continued* participation in a joint enterprise, despite having foreseen the possibility of events turning out as in fact they did. It does not depend upon identifying a coincidence between the wish or agreement of A that an act be done by B and B's doing of that act. The relevant conduct is that of A—in continuing to participate in the venture despite foresight of what may be done by B.[22]

In the instance of publishing zero day threats knowing that attackers will use the code to develop an exploit to commit crimes, it is difficult to see why the doctrine of law of extended common purpose liability should not apply. The publisher of the zero day threat has aided and abetted in the commission of a crime. The foreseeability of criminal use, however, should address whether there is continual cooperation once someone discovers that the zero day threat is being used to commit a crime. This may include cooperation with an anti-virus company or assisting in containing the attack and for forth. Indeed, there is empirical evidence that attacks increase after a vulnerability disclosure.[23] This may be of importance in law. Depending on the jurisdiction in question, a criminal provision may require direct intent while other provisions may only require reasonable foreseeability of the likeliness of an event occurring. Even in the latter case, it will not be enough in law to demonstrate that it was reasonably foreseeable that any public disclosure would increase the risk of attack; it must be proven that *this* public disclosure increased the risk of *this* type of attack. As already seen, if on the same day different security researchers each publish a zero day threat, and that threat is later acted on, it would become difficult to prosecute given that one would likely not know which publication contributed to the attack. Whether a disclosure is responsible may play a role in a legal analysis as will be seen in Sect.4.9.

4.5   Conspiracy to Commit an Offence

Section 11.5 of the *CC* refers to situations where there is conspiracy to commit an offence (punishable by imprisonment for more than 12 months or by a fine of 200 penalty units). Conspiracy requires that there must be an agreement between two or more persons, that the agreement must include intent to commit an offence,

---

[22] *Gillard*, above, paras 117 and 118.

[23] Arora, footnote 16 in Chap. 1.

and that one of the persons must have committed an overt act that was part of the agreement. For instance, if an agreement is made for a hacker to share a newly discovered vulnerability with another person, knowing that the other person will use the vulnerability to commit an offence (such as fraud or other), and that person does indeed carry out the crime, a conspiracy charge could be made. The interesting part of this dilemma is whether the intent to commit a crime might include unauthorised access, modification or impairment. A hacker gives another hacker a security vulnerability knowing that the other hacking will break into the same network, and that network is indeed broken into, all elements of the conspiracy offence are met.

4.6 Possession, Control or Supply of Data/Misuse of a Device

Mere possession, control or supply of data with intent to commit a computer offence such as that found in sections 478.3 and 478.4 (supply) of the *Criminal Code* is not prohibited under the *Convention*. For example, an attacker that collected and stored zero day exploit with the intent of their future use in fraudulent or other illegal activity would be caught under section 478.3 of the *Criminal Code*. The provision applies irrespective of whether the data has been used in an illegal manner (for example fraudulently). The same conduct would not be specifically prohibited under the *Convention*. Articles 4 and 5 of the *Convention* require an illegal use of the data such as deletion or modification. Knowledge and possession of a security vulnerability or exploit could come under this umbrella of the law.

The greatest difference in the computer data provisions lies in article 6 of the *Convention* which prohibits the misuse of a device. This article of the *Convention* enjoys no parallel in the *Criminal Code*. Devices used to illegally access, intercept or interfere with data or computers are not prohibited under the *Criminal Code*. Article 6 of the *Convention* makes illegal the misuse of any device used to commit offences in articles 2–5, and also makes illegal the production, sale, distribution, or making available of such devices. Devices might include a port scanner, or credit card skimmer and may include an exploit. As the definition of device includes a computer program, there is no reason to think that a published exploit would be excluded from this definition. Article 6 could, in theory, apply to the production, sale, or mere making available (publication) of an exploit, especially zero day exploits.

4.6.1 Laws of Misprision/Failure to Report a Serious Crime

Misprision of felony was the offence at common law for failing to report a known felony to the police where, under the circumstances, it was reasonable to do so as well as the reporting was done within reasonable time. Misprision is no longer a common law offence in most jurisdictions including Canada, Australia,

New Zealand, Ireland, England and Wales. Many jurisdictions have, however, enacted legislation establishing an offence for failure to report a serious crime. In Australia, for example, the terms felony and misdemeanour were abolished and replaced with the term "serious crime" and, as such, the common law offence of misprision of felony became moot. In the United States, misprision was codified under 18 U.S.C. §4—Misprision of Felony. American jurisprudence of misprision of felony is rather disparate with some jurisdictions (such as South Carolina) ruling the offence as unsuited to the American criminal law while other jurisdictions (such as Maryland and Virginia), misprision remains an offence.

There are no cases to date addressing misprision and similar legislative provisions in the context of computer security incidents or disclosure of vulnerabilities. The question becomes whether security researchers have a responsibility under the law to report security flaws where such flaws may lead to a serious offence or felony. Misprision has typically meant the reporting of a serious crime to law enforcement. In the computer security world, it is often more important to report vulnerabilities and the possible use of the vulnerability to steal information to the organisation holding the information, the vendor, to anti-virus companies, and other security organisations such as CERTs. These entities are not law enforcement and, therefore, failure to report to such entities would not attract the offense of misprision or its equivalent.

4.7 Security Research Exemption

The *misuse of a device* provision specifically allows nations to provide exemptions for security researchers. It cannot be stressed enough the importance of this type of exemption. Security researchers are not exempt from the computer provisions in all countries included in the Tables in Appendix A. There is an exemption for security research only when the research involves circumventing a technological protection measure, or publishing the circumvention but this is an area of copyright law, and not criminal law per se. Security researchers, organisations, university computer science departments and technology companies are the primary forces behind tackling malware, exploits and illicit Internet activity. For example, in many publicly disclosed botnet take-down instances,[24] security researchers were

---

[24] Pandalabs was heavily involved in the takedown of the Mariposa botnet. Microsoft was heavily involved in the takedown of the Waledac botnet. Law enforcement and a number of international computer security organisations and university researchers aided Microsoft and Pandalabs in the takedown of these botnets. See Jeff Williams, 'Dismantling Waledac' on *Microsoft Malware Protection Centre—Threat Research & Response Blog* (25 February 2010) <http://blogs.technet.com/b/mmpc/archive/2010/02/25/dismantling-waledac.aspx>;   Luis Corrons, 'Mariposa Botnet' on *PandaLabs Blog* (3 March 2010) <http://pandalabs.pandasecurit y.com/mariposa-botnet/>. Technical blogs in the area of Internet security provide the most up-to-date information on security incidents. In this case, the blogs were written by those involved with the take-down of the botnets in question.

heavily involved in spite of the fact that they could have potentially been charged with a form of unauthorised access to computer data. Similarly many security researchers share their work with other researchers in public and semi-public blogs, mailing lists and databases such as VX Heavens, Bugtraq and Metasploit.

4.8 Public Interest Exemption

There is no public interest exemption for computer offences. A public interest exemption refers to unauthorised access, modification or impairment where it is in the public interest to break the law. Typically, this might relate to security research but there are other instances that go beyond mere research which may justify the law being broken. Three examples come to mind. The first involves a publicized identity theft for the purpose of bringing media attention to a serious problem that has been inadequately addressed (if at all) by the appropriate authorities. The second involves an American case related to an anti-spammer. The third case looks at a research organisation dedicated to controlling spam and malware. In many instances of responsible security disclosure it is difficult to see why a public interest exemption should not apply.

4.8.1 Case Study: Bennett Arron

The first example involves a British comedian, Bennett Arron, who was the victim to identity theft and fraud.[25] His dealings with creditors, banks, government entities and law enforcement as a victim led him to become rather dissatisfied with the system. In an effort to publicize just how easy it is to steal an identity due to appalling and absurdly low security prevention measures, he stole the identity of Charles Clarke, the Home Secretary of the United Kingdom. He then produced a television film "How Not to Lose Your Identity" for Channel 4. Bennett was able to not only steal the Home Secretary's identity but he did so with minimal effort in only a few short weeks; he required a razor blade and Google skills. No hacking was involved. He was arrested shortly after the release of the film and the charges were then later dropped. He became famous in the UK and was heralded by many newspapers as a hero for this documentary. His fame even included an appearance on the Australian SBS programme, INSIGHT.[26]

---

[25] For more information about Bennett Arron see http://en.wikipedia.org/wiki/Bennett_Arron (last accessed May 31, 2010).

[26] SBS, Insight "Stolen ID" available at http://news.sbs.com.au/insight/episode/index/id/30 (last accessed May 29, 2010).

4.8.2 Case Study: Sierra v. Ritz

The US trial court decision of *Sierra v. Ritz*[27] involved unauthorised use of a domain name system zone transfer. Zone transfers are, generally speaking, open access public information.[28] They provide data about all of the machines within a domain. Without zone transfer, you would literally have to type in an IP (internet protocol) address every time you went to a website—it is one factor contributing to the convenience of the Internet. Zone transfer are not, however, necessary infrastructure to the Internet and have, in fact, increasingly become disabled for security reasons. The information may be retrieved by the use of 'host command' with the 'l' option. Zone transfers contain public information to varying degrees depending on the protocols used by an organization. Zone transfers may be disabled to the greater public with only trusted machines and senior administrators having access on a 'need to know' basis. This is a form of limited authorised public access. In Sierra's case, the zone transfer was more widely available in the sense that the system allowed zone transfers to everyone, thereby publicizing potentially private data into a public forum. There would be no way for a person accessing the zone transfer in the latter context to know whether Sierra was truly allowing shared access or whether it was merely a mis-configuration. From a technical perspective, this is a situation of authorised access to the information found in the zone transfer. From a legal perspective, the judge ruled that access was unauthorised with a large emphasis placed on the defendant's intention to obtain and divulge information found in the zone transfer.[29] David Ritz is a well-known anti-spammer. There has been debate as to whether Sierra has facilitated spam in the past. Neither of these two facts appeared to weigh into the decision. While *Sierra v. Ritz* is a civil suit, Ritz has been criminally charged with unauthorised access to a computer in North Dakota. The criminal trial is pending.

The case illustrates how the terms 'unauthorised' and 'access' do not produce a similar set of shared assumptions in the technical, legal or ethical fields. A technical researcher may falsely assume that they are operating within safe legal parameters only to discover that such parameters do not translate across fields. The technical researcher would likely assume that he/she is authorised to perform an act where technical protocols and programming convention allow for it. From a legal standpoint, authorisation and consent involve a number of factors including intention, damage, and the bargaining position of affected parties. One commentator on the decision noted that it is the equivalent of, "Mommy, *can* I have a

---

[27] The judgment is unreported. A copy of the decision is accessible from private list-serves as well as from the webpages of SpamSuite.com. *Sierra Corporate Design Inc. v. David Ritz*, (2007) District Court, County of Cass, State of North Dakota, File No. op-05-C-01660 *See* www.spamsuit.com.com/node/351.

[28] The analysis is largely based on this article by the author [4].

[29] A detailed analysis of the case can be found on SpamSuite.com available at http://www.spamsuite.com/node/351.

cookie? Sure you can have a cookie, but you *may* not".[30] The case foregrounds a recurring theme: if a user interacts with a server in a way that the protocol does not prohibit but which is upsetting to the server's operator, should this be construed as "unauthorised access" as a matter of law?[31] The scope of unauthorised access in computer fraud statutes is an old question.[32] The novelty stems from looking an unauthorised access from a public interest perspective.

Exemption from liability and criminal prosecution has been argued for application to white hacking, and for acts that threaten to cross technical and accepted protocols. A resounding question underlies the debate: do the ends justify the means? Some examples might include the Recording Industry's proposal to hack into users' computers to find infringing material and cyber-activists placing Trojans on child pornography to track and record the contents of offenders hard-drives for evidential purposes. These examples go to the question of intent as well as whether or not an act may be justified as social utility for the good of the public similar to how public interest exemptions work for the admissibility or otherwise inadmissible evidence in court.

If one argues that David Ritz has indeed accessed the zone transfer without authorization, inevitably one must question his motive, intent and whether such activities were performed in the public interest. Peering into the zone transfer to document illegal spamming activity may indeed be in the public interest. If one successfully concludes that no unauthorised access was performed due to the public nature of the zone transfer and DNS, it seems equally perverse to not consider motive and intent. By way of analogy, if I have equipment to make false passports along with a stack of 200 shell passports (no photos or false names inserted), the trajectory towards the commission of a crime is called into question. Accessing information in the zone transfer for illicit purposes should attract attention, if not a penalty. The implication, however, of criminalizing an act of accessing publicly available information without illicit intent, calls into question the utility of 'unauthorised access' provisions. The inconsistency of the courts' interpretation of 'unauthorised access' makes the use of the provision unpredictable as well as malleable to prosecutorial will. The scope of 'unauthorised access' is ripe for reconsideration and debate.

4.8.3 Case Study: Spamhaus Project

Spamhaus Project, an organisation of volunteers in the computer industry, composes blacklists of some of the worst spam propagators to aid ISPs and businesses to better filter spam. The company E360insight.com sued Spamhaus Project in the Northern District of Illinois Federal Court alleging it was a legally operating direct

---

[30] [5].

[31] Original idea expressed by Paul Ohm in the cyberprof list serve.

[32] *See* Orin Kerr's seminal article on unauthorised access [6].

marketing company and should not be blacklisted as a spam provider. Spamhaus did not file a response and did not appear before the court. As such, the arguments presented before the court were unilateral such that the court issued a default judgment.[33] The court ordered Spamhaus to pay $11.7 million USD, to post a notice that E360 was not a spammer, and ordered that the Spamhaus Internet address be removed from the Internet Corporation for Assigned Names and Numbers (ICANN). Spamhaus ignored the ruling, did not pay the money, and did not post a notice on its website that E360 was not a spammer, nor did ICANN remove the Spamhaus website from its root server. In a similar situation, the anti-virus and anti-spyware company Symantec was taken to court in California by a company which it defines and reports in its services as spyware. Hotbar.com claims that the classification of its software as spyware is in violation of trade libel laws, and constitutes interference with contract. The suit was reported as settled with Symantec agreeing to classify Hotbar as 'low risk'.[34] A series of cases of a similar nature have been filed and heard between 2005 and 2009, with most settling.[35]

There are compelling reasons in these instances to allow for a public interest exemption. However, in my opinion these reasons are not sufficiently compelling at this point in time as to open up the exemption beyond security research. The idea of a public interest exemption, however, should be given further consideration by governments.

4.9 Possible "Responsible Disclosure" Factors and Their Relation with the Law

The only absolute in this area of law is that it is unsettled, therefore, any legal advice would tell you that any type of security disclosure could expose you to criminal sanction and civil liability. However, we must always believe that the application of law is reasonable and that there are many mitigating factors that the legal system would take into account either when choosing to prosecute, selecting the crime to charge one with, in the final judgement, and whether or not any sentence would be given. The following factors may contribute to a legal analysis.

- whether or not a vulnerability is published;
- whether the publication is partial or full;
- publication venue; and
- recipients of publication

---

[33] *E360 Insight, LLC* et al. *v. The Spamhaus Projec,t* US District Court, Norther District of Illinois, 13 September 2006 (Case no. 06 C 3958). Access to default judgment at http://www.spamhaus.org/archive/legal/Kocoras_order_to_Spamhaus.pdf.

[34] Messmer 2006.

[35] *1-800 Contacts v WhenU., 1-800 Solutions v. Zone Labs, Cassav (CasinoOnNet) v Sunbelt Software, Claria (Gator) v Internet Advertising Bureau.*

Whether or not a vulnerability is published must be differentiated between the disclosure of a vulnerability. For example, responsible disclosure might include letting the software vendor know of a bug in their system, or letting all anti-virus software producers know of the vulnerability. As seen in the case study of Patrick Webster in Sect. 2.1.1 even this type of limited disclosure can result in legal action.

Disclosure may be partial or in full. As seen in the partial disclosure in the Cisco router case, the law is not interested in whether the disclosure is partial or full. In this instance, Cisco was concerned about the publication venue and the recipients of the publication. Demonstrating a flaw in one of the world's leading routers at the world's largest hacker conference played a stronger role than whether disclosure was partial or full.

The publication venue is important and ties in directly with the recipients of publication as the venue more or less indicates who the likely recipients of information will be. Metasploits, for example, is a publicly accessible website but access to its zero day exploits is limited to those who sign-up, and therefore have a username and password. This is a way for the site's owners to ascertain who is receiving information about the exploits. Though one may query the effectiveness of a username and password system, especially when dealing with people whose skill set is that of deception and identity fraud.

References

1. Maurushat A (2010) Australia's accession to the cybercrime convention: is the convention relevant in combating cybercrime in the era of botnets and obfuscation crime tools? 16(1)
2. Protalinkski E (2012) British student jailed for hacking into Facebook. 18 Feb 2012 available at http://www.zdnet.com/blog/facebook/british-student-jailed-for-hacking-into-facebook/9244
3. Mangham G (2012) The Facebook Hack: What Really Happened. 23 April, 2012 available at http://gmangham.blogspot.co.uk/2012/04/facebook-hack-what-really-happened.html
4. Maurushat A, Yu R (2009) When internet protocols and legal provisions collide: unauthorised access and sierra v. Ritz. Comput Law Secur Rev 25(2):185–188
5. Rash M (2008) Mother, May I. available at http://www.securityfocus.com/print/columnists/463. (last Accessed 29 Jan 2008)
6. Kerr O (2003) Cybercrime's scope: interpreting 'access' and 'authorization' in computer misuse statutes. NY Univ Law Rev 78(3):1596–1668

Chapter 5
Other Legal and Ethical Issues

Abstract This chapter considers legal areas outside the scope of criminal law. Civil liability and civil liberties are discussed in the context of security disclosure. These are: freedom of expression/free speech, copyright, tort of negligence, defamation, illegal telecommunications interception (surveillance), privacy law, data protection and data breach notification.

5.1 Introduction

Computer offences remain the main area of law in the disclosure of security vulnerabilities. There are a number of other areas, however, that have some relevance. These include freedom of expression/free speech, copyright, tort of negligence, defamation, illegal telecommunication interceptions, privacy law, data protection and data breach notification.

5.1.1 Freedom of Expression/Free Speech

Is there a right of free speech to disclose a security vulnerability? The answer to this question is highly contextual.

Generally, freedom of expression has meant the freedom to publish, which in turn includes the freedom to speak, write and print.[1] More liberal and broad interpretations include the right to communicate as well as to receive (or not receive) content. Freedom of expression is a right protected in a number of international human rights treaties, as well as a legally entrenched domestic right in many jurisdictions in the world, and is considered by many to be a universal moral right. Many theories exist to justify freedom of expression. The utilitarian theory of free speech espouses the idea that speech is a tool to advance truth, democracy and the exchange of ideas.[2] The libertarian model seeks to protect

---

[1] This section borrows from Aycock and Maurushat [1].

[2] [2].

A. Maurushat, *Disclosure of Security Vulnerabilities*, SpringerBriefs in Cybersecurity,   53
DOI: 10.1007/978-1-4471-5004-6_5, © The Author(s) 2013

individual self-determination rather than any right.[3] Other frameworks such as Asian values would conceptualise freedom of expression as a narrow concept confined to duties owed to a community—one which does not extend to individual rights.[4] No matter what theory one subscribes to, freedom of expression or free speech, has never been absolute. Public, private and self-censorship as well as other limitations look to restrain free speech where it is deemed potentially harmful to society.[5]

Is the publication of existing vulnerabilities, zero day threats and future threats harmful to society? The answer remains untested or at least unquantified. The answer also returns to the debate of security of obscurity and full disclosure. Disclosure may allow defences to be in place before threats are released to the wild. Communication of new threats under the "commons model" may further allow for the superior defences to be adopted. Under the commons model, knowledge and information are shared. Sharing of information and resources is based on the premise that, by having the opportunity to build on each other's ideas, rather than duplicate one another's efforts in a "closed" environment, security vendors are able to produce more efficient and technologically secure products. Conversely, disclosure may allow for an otherwise unknown threat to be released (if not certainly expedited) to the wild.

Freedom of expression arguments become interesting where such expression intersects with legislative provisions, and in particular, criminal law. Legislation which unduly impairs freedom of expression may be struck down as unconstitutional by the courts (not in all jurisdictions but available as a defence in, for example, Canada, the United States and the European Union). When expression, in this case a computer program, becomes an integral part of a crime, a freedom of expression defence will likely be foreclosed unless there is evidence that the expression is directed at ideas remote from the commission of a criminal act.[6] For this reason, a person or group who writes but does not disseminate malware, then makes it available to the public, will likely not be able to rely on freedom of expression as a defence. The publication of future threats or zero day threats such as a hacker at a conference would likely present a closer nexus to becoming part of a future crime, than merely an idea. The disclosure of a zero day threat or future threat research at a security conference, however, is less ambiguous and would likely be more aligned with presenting ideas. These thoughts are generalizations as all such legal analysis is highly fact-specific.

---

[3] [3].

[4] [4].

[5] [5].

[6] see Ref. [5].

5.1.2 Copyright

Disclosure of security vulnerabilities may involve potential breaches to copyright law.[7] Where a copy of even a portion of computer code is reproduced (in some cases even RAM will suffice) the conduct may result in copyright infringement. Where a technological protection measure (TPM) or digital rights management (DRM) system is used, the mere act of circumvention will result in an additional infringement.

A famous example of circumvention of a TPM involved Professor Edward Felten and his colleagues when they published and presented their research in the successful breaking of the digital watermark copy prevention on music files otherwise known as SDMI.[8] The circumvention was performed as part of the "Hack SDMI Challenge" where the recording industry challenged the public to test the security of proposed SDMI copy prevention systems. Felten's team circumvented a number of the SDMI protection mechanisms. In order to claim a prize for successfully breaking these codes, Felten and his team would have had to agree not to disclose the technical details of their circumvention solutions.[9]

The Felten team opted to publish their results instead of accepting the prize. The SDMI member companies sent Felten's team a letter threatening actions under the anti-circumvention measures in the United States Digital Millennium Copyright Act. Concerned that it could be subject to criminal liability if it allowed the Felten paper to be presented at its security conference, the USENIX technical conference organisation became involved. After a large amount of negative publicity, the recording industry withdrew their opposition to the presentation of the paper.

Most jurisdictions' laws on copyright contain what is known as fair use (United States—exception rights) or fair dealings (Commonwealth and many civil law countries such as France, Canada, the United Kingdom, Australia—defences to copyright infringement. Research and in particular encryption research is an exception or defence to copyright infringement in many jurisdictions, as is the ability to reverse engineer software for interoperability purposes.[10] The problem, however, lies in who is entitled to the exception or defence. Universities are clear cut examples of falling within the parameters of fair use or dealings. Hackers who do not have authorization to "ethically" hack into a system would not be entitled to this exception or defense. When disclosure of a vulnerability involves reproducing all or part of the software code, publication by a hacker will likely be copyright infringement. The security and reverse engineering exceptions will likely not apply. As we move towards technology companies and anti-virus vendors disclosure the line is less clear cut.

---

[7] This section is based on Refs. [1] and [6].

[8] [6].

[9] See footnote 8.

[10] [7].

To add to this dilemma, many jurisdictions allow companies to contract out of fair dealing provisions. For example, it is common to open up proprietary software containing an end user license agreement which prevents the user from reverse engineering the code. One countermeasure is found in jurisdictions which have the defence of "in the public interest". It could readily be argued that the publication of security vulnerabilities, and in particular zero day threats and future threats, would be considered as an integral component in effectively combating high-tech crime. It would be difficult to counter this argument where disclosure was made to a closed venue such as the anti-virus community, where the actual computer code is not revealed, and where there are potentially great benefits from disclosing.

Copyright law generally contains both civil and criminal provisions. While there may not be political will to prosecute security vendors and those who disclose vulnerabilities, the threat of civil liability is less predictable as a wider range of parties may bring suit, all of who may be motivated by a variety of factors.

In a somewhat different fashion copyright may also come to the forefront in the disclosure of malware code. Malware writers released an amusing copyright license with their malware product. See the image below courtesy of Symantec Fig. 5.1.[11]

Symantec had the license translated from Russian into English. According to clause 4, the user of the malware program, "Does not have the right to deliberately send any portion of the product to anti-virus companies and other such institutions." Clause 2 further specifies that the customer, "May not disassemble/study the binary code of the bot builder." These clauses can be interpreted as not giving rise to a right to disclose the code or the security vulnerability that the malicious software exploits whereby, "In case of violations of the agreement and being detected, the client loses any technical support. Moreover, the binary code of your bot will be immediately sent to antivirus companies."

The license is more amusing than it is helpful in demonstrating the copyright position of disclosure.

5.1.3 Tort of Negligence/Delict

Where a person or entity presented a security flaw that he or she knew or ought to have reasonably known would result in its release to the wild (or expedition of), there is the possibility of a civil suit in negligence (Common law),[12] delict[13] (civil law jurisdictions where there is intention) or quasi-delict if the result is unintentional (civil law jurisdictions).

---

[11] [8].

[12] *See generally* [9].

[13] *See generally* [10].

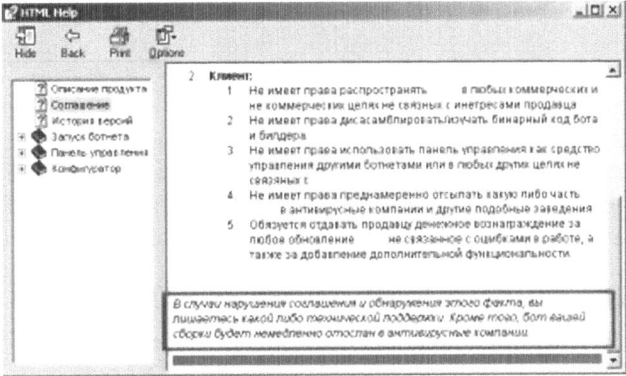

1. Does not have the right to distribute the product in any business or commercial purposes not connected with this sale.
2. May not disassemble / study the binary code of the bot builder.
3. Has no right to use the control panel as a means to control other bot nets or use it for any other purpose.
4. Does not have the right to deliberately send any portion of the product to anti-virus companies and other such institutions.
5. Commits to give the seller a fee for any update to the product that is not connected with errors in the work, as well as for adding additional functionality.

These are typical restrictions that could be applied to any software product, legitimate or not. However, the most interesting part of the agreement is the section marked in red in the above screen shot:

In cases of violations of the agreement and being detected, the client loses any technical support. Moreover, the binary code of your bot will be immediately sent to antivirus companies.

Fig. 5.1 Software license for Malware with humorous copyright provisions

In order for an act in negligence to succeed, it must be shown that there was a duty of care between the parties, and that physical damage was sustained. In the case of publication, there would not normally be a duty of care in the common law between, for example, a conference presenter and the victim of a malicious attack. As one expert writes, "Under the common law of negligence, a novel duty of care is only usually imposed by the courts where it is reasonably foreseeable that a failure in that duty would cause damage to the person to whom the duty is owed, and where there is no good policy reason to reduce or limit that liability.[14] This is known as the remoteness test.

The civil law principle differs in that there is a universal principle of civil responsibility. Expressed in a different way, a duty of care is owed to everyone. Civil law generally recognizes three components: fault, damage and causation. Remoteness or proximity is factored in at the level of causation and the amount of damages awarded (if any). Future threats may be seen as too remote to have caused a threat to be released into the wild. An existing or zero day threat, however, would likely not be seen as too remote. Causation would be difficult to prove in court.

---

[14] [11].

The tort of negligence or delict is also potentially applicable to the recipients of information on the security vulnerability. Where a vendor or company is made aware of a security flaw, then deliberately chooses to ignore the fact by not fixing the bug, negligence or delict could apply. So inaction or failure to act may also trigger negligence. In this situation where the vendor has a direct client relationship with the affected end user, the proximity test is easily made. Further action could possibly also be taken in this circumstance under the law of contracts.

Some exploit sharing communities such as Metasploit have a legal defence fund in place to aid their contributors in the event that criminal charges are laid and for civil liability suits.[15]

5.1.4 Defamation

Defamation law may be governed under civil law codes, by legislation and by common law principles. The main issue in defamation relates to how a person's reputation is protected over the right of free speech. In Australia for example free speech in the political arena is implied into the constitution but is not a protected right. This is different to the United States, Canada and most countries in Europe where freedom of speech enjoys broader constitutional protection. Under Australian law, a person may bring a defamation case based on information posted by someone outside of Australia providing that the material is accessed in Australia and that the defamed person enjoyed a reputation in Australia. By American standards this could be conceived as libel tourism. However, a different viewpoint is that jurisdictions such as the United Kingdom and Australia utilize a different legal test for defamation, and a different balance between the right to reputation and freedom of expression.

There are several general principles in defamation.[16] First, there must be publicised defamatory statements (e.g. cartoon, audio recording, article, website) either about a person, organisation or company. Second, the statements must be damaging to a person's or organisation's reputation. Third, the reputation must be diminished in the eyes of one's peers.

- The statement/imputation must have a defamatory meaning
- It must identify the plaintiff
- It must have been published
- Damage to reputation of the plaintiff

---

[15] Correspondence with contributor to Metasploit.

[16] For a general overview of defamation law see Gillooly [12].

The author, editor, printer, publisher, broadcaster, distributor, website moderator, Internet Service Provider, and employer can all be potentially sued in defamation. Defences to defamation include:

- Truth or Fair comment (public interest)
- Innocent Disseminator
- Absolute & Qualified Privilege
- Protected Publications

Remedies to defamation typically include:

- Removal of defamatory materials/injunction which prevents party from publishing or re-publishing materials
- Money/compensation
- Public apology or retraction

Defamation may also be criminal in some jurisdictions. France and Australia, for example, still have criminal provisions for defamation. Criminal defamation charges have also been filed over online content. Adelaide teenager Christopher Cross was convicted in November 2009 of criminal defamation for comments he posted on Facebook about a police officer. Cross was convicted and placed on a two-year and AUD $500 good behaviour bond. If Cross breaches the bond he could conceivably face up to three years in jail.[17]

Interestingly, there is no known caselaw of hackers suing one another in defamation though one would think that this would be an area rife for the picking. Hackers often comment on the work of other hackers in forums and blogs; reputation is of considerable importance in this community. Such comments might entail discussion on a security vulnerability, an exploit, malware, and so forth. As seen in the example of a security researcher and McAfee in Sect. 3.4, the researcher was very concerned about his reputation as a programmer, and his reputation in general. The listing of the programmer's website on the pornography blacklist could be construed as defamation. Every requirement of defamation is met. However, in that situation McAfee retracted the classification, apologised, and removed the offending classification.

5.1.5 Illegal Telecommunications Interception (Surveillance)

Some security vulnerabilities may be discovered through the interception of telecommunications data. For instance, one may want to intercept email and mobile phone conversation between security personnel in a corporation such as Microsoft or Cisco. Albeit a remote method of vulnerability discovery, there are some legal issues which need to be examined. Most jurisdictions sanction the interception and

---

[17] [13].

examination of communications. This includes 'communications' which would be considered information such as an email as it passes over the Internet from one point to another, 'stored communications' where communications when they are not passing over a telecommunications system and where they are held by a carrier, such as an ISP that stores the email content, and data logs which provide information about points in a communication trail such as the storage of telephone records, internet traffic and transaction data. Telecommunications legislation is the source of frequent amendments. As a general rule some types of entities such as Internet Service Providers and Telephone Companies are permitted to intercept data in specific contexts such as in the interest of national security and network protection. This may include by warrant and data retention laws requiring an ISP to maintain data logs. Security researchers are not exempt from interception laws.

5.1.6 Privacy Law

Privacy law varies considerably from country to country. In general, the tort of invasion of privacy or privacy intrusion is available in Commonwealth countries. However, the law in some Commonwealth countries has yet to allow claims for this tort. New Zealand, most provinces in Canada, and Ireland all recognise the tort of invasion of privacy.

The tort of invasion of privacy requires that several conditions are met: reasonable expectation of privacy, highly offensive invasion of privacy, the public interest, and a requirement of fault.[18]

Should the act of discovering and disclosing a vulnerability inadvertently invade the privacy of individuals, it is possible but not probable that the tort of invasion of privacy would apply. Certainly there would be an expectation of privacy for most forms of held personal information. Additionally the requirement of fault is likely meant if there was intent to invade privacy or if a party was reckless. It would be difficult, however, to demonstrate that the act was highly invasive given that the purpose is to expose deficient security and vulnerabilities in networks and products. In fact, in some instances this might be seen as public interest service. As this tort has not yet been used in the context of security disclosure, it is difficult to predict whether it is a genuine legal concern for security researchers.

The United Kingdom does not recognise privacy torts. The doctrine of breach of confidence is used instead. This doctrine is also actionable in Canada, Australia and New Zealand. Breach of confidence involves the improper publication of information obtained or given in confidence that ought not to be divulged. Here there has to be some form of publication or use of confidential information. Many cases involve disclosure of confidential health information about famous people.[19]

---

[18] *See* [14].

[19] For example, [15].

Most security disclosures will not publish personal information or confidential information. If they did, it would be ancillary and likely would not meet the requirements of breach of confidence.

Four privacy torts are available in the United States:

1. Intrusion upon seclusion or solitude, or into private affairs;
2. Public disclosure of embarrassing private facts;
3. Publicity which places a person in a false light in the public eye; and
4. Appropriation of name or likeness.

The right to recover damages for invasion of privacy is well established in American law. The above four torts were first espoused in a famous essay, "The Right to Privacy", in the 1890 by Warren and Brandeis.[20] The first two torts are potentially relevant to security disclosure where personal information is intruded upon. The second tort, public disclosure requires the information disclosed to be embarrassing (somewhat remote in the context of security disclosure). The first, intrusion is most relevant with the specifics found in The Restatement (Second) or Torts.

The Restatement (Second) of Torts §652B provides:

> One who intentionally intrudes, physically or otherwise, upon the solitude or seclusion of another or his private affairs or concerns, is subject to liability to the other for invasion of his privacy, if the intrusion would be highly offensive to a reasonable person.

A claimant must plead and prove four elements:[21]

1. there was an unauthorized intrusion or prying into his seclusion;
2. the intrusion was highly offensive to or objectionable to a reasonable person;
3. the matter intruded upon was private; and
4. the intrusion caused anguish and suffering.

These elements are similar to the requirements in Commonwealth countries for the tort of invasion of privacy, and the same reasoning with respect to security disclosure would apply.

5.1.7 Data Protection

Data protection laws are legislatively or administratively based. Most jurisdictions have adopted data protection rules for corporations and organisations that collect and use personal information. The only legal method for security researchers to collect data (whether intentionally or unintentionally) is to have their consent. This is usually done through a privacy policy. Security researchers may, as seen in the example of Patrick Webster, discover a vulnerability and in doing so have

---

[20] [16].

[21] *See generally*, [17].

accessed and copied personal information. The accessing and storing of personal information while discovering the vulnerability may be automatically part of the running code. Nonetheless, the law is clear that you need permission to access or store this data. Obviously a security researcher is not going to notify and obtain consent to access this data as this is not an integral or even important component in identifying vulnerabilities. Nonetheless the security researcher should be aware that accessing, using or storing personal information, no matter what the intention, may have direct affect on the organisation who holds the information under what is known as data security principles.

Security principles found in privacy instruments generally require organizations to take reasonable measures from misuse and loss of personal information, as well as from unauthorised access, modification or disclosure of data. In principle, data security principles are focused on preventing security incidents by requiring organizations to take reasonable steps to secure data. In theory, therefore, such principles are preventative in nature. Typically, a security blunder is made, the Privacy Commissioner or relevant authority, decides whether or not to investigate a complaint, in some instances the complaint is investigated and a report with a series of recommendations for the organization is made in the hope of preventing further violations. In operation, the principle works as a response to security breaches.

There are a number of security standards and guidelines that have been developed over the years including: The OECD's Information Security Guidelines (1992 and 2002).[22] The 1992 frameworks calls on member states to implement regulation such as criminal and administrative provisions for the misuse and abuse of information systems. The goal is to provide a minimum standard for security of information systems. Unlike the 1992 *Security of Information System Guidelines*, the more recent 2002 *Security Guidelines* are comprised with a set of principles which do not request member states to act in any specific fashion and, in particular, no heed is paid to incorporating the principles into domestic law and regulation.

The *Security Guidelines* discuss nine core principles: (1) Awareness—Participants should incorporate security as an essential element of information systems, (2) Responsibility—All participants are responsible for the security of information systems and networks, (3) Response—Participants should act in a timely and co-operative manner to prevent, detect and respond to security incidents, (4) Ethics—Participants should respect the legitimate interests of others, (5) Democracy—The security of information systems and networks should be compatible with essential values of a democratic society, (6) Risk assessment—Participants should conduct risk assessments, (7) Security design and implementation—Participants should incorporate security as an essential element of information systems and networks, (8) Security management—Participants should adopt a comprehensive approach to security management, and (9) Reassessment—Participants should review and reassess the security of information systems and

---

[22] [18].

networks, and make appropriate modifications to security policies, practices, measures and procedures. These Guidelines, however, do not offer useful information for security management for data loss and damage as the result of exploit, malware, or any form of unauthorised access.

5.1.8 Data Breach Notification

Security research and disclosure which has the ancillary effect of having accessed and compromised personal data may inadvertently force a company to notify all affected parties that their data has been breached.

Data breach notification and disclosure laws are emerging around the globe. In essence, data breach notification legally requires corporations and organisations to notify individuals when a breach of security leads to the disclosure of personal information.[23] Two related phrases aptly describe the impetus behind such laws: *"Sunlight as disinfectant"* and the *"Right to Know"*. Data breach notification is promulgated under the theory that the consumer has the right to know when *their* personal information has been stolen or compromised. Equally, it is hoped that data breach notification laws will provide a necessary incentive for corporations and organizations to take adequate steps to secure personal information held within their organization. In this sense, exposing security breaches of corporations will shine "sunlight" onto an organization's security practices, and will "disinfect" those problematic security areas requiring change.

The scope of such notification and disclosure schemes varies greatly from country to country. Many jurisdictions such as the United States, the European Union and Australia have tabled Bills or passed Acts legislating mandatory data breach disclosure. Other jurisdictions such as Canada and Japan have instituted voluntary guidelines. In many jurisdictions, data breach notification is currently sector specific (Eg. banking and financial sector or the telecommunications sector).[24] Many of the current proposals, guidelines, and laws take from the experience of the United States, most notably with California which in 2002 passed strict data breach notification laws. Jurisdictions borrowing from the American experience have gained insight into aspects from some of these initial laws. However, some elements from current proposals in Australia, Canada and the EU highlight and ignore problematic aspects of the U.S. legislation.

Though security researchers may strongly believe that full disclosure incentivises better security practices, they may not realise that such disclosures may come at great personal cost to an organisation. Corporations and organisations in most jurisdictions are required to notify users if their personal data has been breached

---

[23] The idea comes from a paper written by Romanosky et al. [19].

[24] For an examination of data breach notification laws from over 30 jurisdictions see Maurushat [20].

under data breach notification rules. Empirical work on how much data breach notification costs organisations has been carried out by Ponemon Institute. Their latest report finds that:

> The study found the average organizational cost per data breach was $5.5 million in 2011, down 24 percent from $7.2 million in 2010. Additionally, the cost per compromised record fell to $194 per record, down $20 (10 percent) from 2010.[25]

The argument may exist that the organisation wouldn't have to comply with data breach notification laws had they been properly securing customer data in the first place. While this is true to a certain extent, the aim of the law was to improve security from third parties with malicious purpose and not against ethical security researchers. Nonetheless, the costs of data breach notification are not so insignificant that security researchers and hackers can merely shrug this off once full disclosure is made, and there is evidence that personal data has been breached.

References

1. Aycock J, Maurushat A (2007) Future threats. In: Virus bulletin conference
2. Moon R (2000) The constitutional protection of freedom of expression. University of Toronto Press, Toronto
3. Barendt E (2005) Freedom of speech, 2nd edn. Oxford University Press, Oxford
4. Maurushat A (2007) The benevolent health worm: comparing Western human-rights based ethics and confucius duty-based moral philosophy" In: Computer ethics: philosophical enquiry conference (CEPE 2007)
5. Colangelo A, Maurushat A (2006) "Exploring the limits of computer code as a protected form of expression: a suggested approach to encryption, computer viruses and technological protection measures" 1 McGill Law J 51: 47
6. Kerr I, Tacit C, Maurushat A (2002–2003) Technical protection measures: tilting at copyright's windmill (2002–2003) vol. 34 Ottawa Law Review No. 1
7. Bambauer Derek E, Oliver D (2010) The hacker's aegis (March 1 2010). Brooklyn Law School, Legal Studies Paper No. 184. Available at SSRN: http://ssrn.com/abstract=1561845 or http://dx.doi.org/10.2139/ssrn.1561845
8. Symantec Blog (2010) available at http://www.symantec.com/connect/blogs/copyright-violations-underground
9. Fleming J G (1998) The law of Torts 9th ed, L/KN30
10. Baudoin, Jobin (2005) Les obligations, 6th ed. Éditions Yvon Blais, Cowansville
11. Chandler J (2004) Security in cyberspace: combating distributed denial of service attacks. Univ Ottawa Law and Technol J 1(1–2):231–261
12. Gillooly M (1998) The law of defamation in Australia and New Zealand, Federation Press
13. Hunt N (2009) Teen guilty of facebook slur, Sunday Mail (SA). http://www.adelaidenow.com.au/news/south-australia/teen-guilty-of-facebook-slur/story-e6frea83-1225801651074. 22 Nov 2009
14. Walker S (2000) Media law: commentary and materials. LBC, UK
15. *Campbell v. Mirror Group Newspaper Ltd* (2004) UKHL 22
16. Warren and Brandeis (1890) The right to privacy, 4 Harvard law review 193

---

[25] [21].

17. Solove DJ, Marc R, Schwartz PM (2006) Privacy, information, and technology. Aspen Publishers, Alphen
18. OECD (1992) Security of information system guidelines, and 2002 security guidelines available at http://www.oecd.org/document/42/0,3343,en_2649_34255_15582250_1_1_1_1,00.html
19. Romanosky S, Telang R, Acquisti A (2008) Do data breach disclosure laws reduce identity theft? In: Seventh workshop on the economics of information security, June 2008. These phrases are attributable to Justice Louis Brandeis 1933. http://www.brandeis.edu/investigate/sunlight. Accessed 30 Jan 2009
20. Maurushat A (2009) Data breach notification law across the world from California to Australia UNSWLRS 11
21. Ponemon Institute (2011) Global cost of a data breach (2010) available at http://www.ponemon.org/data-security

Chapter 6
Conclusion

Abstract The concluding chapter addresses responsible disclosure. In doing so, the author is looking at ways forward in computer security to provide incentive to improve the security of products, as well as to enable security researchers a legal method of finding and reporting vulnerabilities such as a security research exemption.

While there are many internet enthusiasts and computer programmers with opinions on computer security, few are as entertaining or as relevant as Linus Torvalds, pioneer of the Linux operating system used all over the world, including Google and android platforms. In an interview with Wired magazine, Torvald discusses the security industry and security researchers:

> The economics of the security world are all horribly nasty, and are largely based on fear, intimidation and blackmail. It's why I compared them to the TSA—even when you know there are morons that didn't finish high school and are stealing camera equipment and harassing people with ridiculous rules, you can't actually speak up against them because there's no recourse.
>
> …
>
> I'm occasionally impressed by the things some of the people do—especially the people finding some *really* obscure way to take some innocent-looking bug and turn it into an exploit—but then in order to take advantage of their discovery they have to take that really interesting intellectual exercise and turn it into this really sordid affair. It's either some (very) thinly veiled blackmail behind some 'best security practices' bullshit, or it's a carefully orchestrated PR event with the timing set so that they look important and interesting.[1]

It is not hard to imagine how Torvald would characterise those in the industry who sell vulnerabilities to corporations for huge profits. If we don't subscribe to Torvald's sordid views of the security industry and security researchers as "best security practices bullshit", and the view that security vulnerability disclosure may improve security practices, the question then becomes what constitutes responsible disclosure.

A number of ethical codes of conduct exist regarding disclosure of security vulnerabilities. One of the first policies was written by a hacker known as Rain Forest Puppy (RFP) who was one of the most respected hackers and researchers in the field due to what is now considered his ethical and even-handed approach

---

[1] [1].

to disclosure of vulnerabilities. RFP wrote a guideline on ethical disclosure of vulnerabilities—how researchers should deal with vendors once a vulnerability is discovered.

The original RFPolicy was published on www.wiretrip.net/rfp/policy.html with copies replicated on multiple websites. The executive summary of the policy is:

Executive overview for vendors and software maintainers

This policy states the 'guidelines' that an individual intends to follow. You basically have 5 days (read below for the definitions and semantics of what is considered a 'day') to return contact to the individual, and must keep in contact with them *at least* every 5 days. Failure to do so will discourage them from working with you and encourage them to publicly disclose the security problem.

This policy is not set in stone–in fact, it is encouraged that all parties regularly communicate with each during the process, adjusting as situations arise.[2]

Zero Day Initiative (ZDI) also has produced a policy on responsible disclosure. ZDI's policy is similar to that of RFPolicy with more specific indications of how to communicate with the affected vendor:

This policy outlines how HP DVLabs handles responsible vulnerability disclosure to product vendors, HP TippingPoint customers, security vendors and the general public. HP DVLabs will responsibly and promptly notify the appropriate product vendor of a security flaw with their product(s) or service(s). The first attempt at contact will be through any appropriate contacts or formal mechanisms listed on the vendor Web site, or by sending an e-mail to security@, support@, info@, and secure@company.com with the pertinent information about the vulnerability. Simultaneous with the vendor being notified, DVLabs may distribute vulnerability protection filters to its customers' IPS devices through the Digital Vaccine service.

If a vendor fails to acknowledge DVLabs initial notification within five business days, DVLabs will initiate a second formal contact by a direct telephone call to a representative for that vendor. If a vendor fails to respond after an additional five business days following the second notification, DVLabs may rely on an intermediary to try to establish contact with the vendor. If DVLabs exhausts all reasonable means in order to contact a vendor, then DVLabs may issue a public advisory disclosing its findings fifteen business days after the initial contact.

If a vendor response is received within the timeframe outlined above, DVLabs will allow the vendor 6-months to address the vulnerability with a patch. At the end of the deadline if a vendor is not responsive or unable to provide a reasonable statement as to why the vulnerability is not fixed, the ZDI will publish a limited advisory including mitigation in an effort to enable the defensive community to protect the user. We believe that by doing so the vendor will understand the responsibility they have to their customers and will react appropriately.[3]

The CERT/CC Vulnerability Disclosure Policy echoes many of the themes in the Zero Day Initiative policy with some small differences.[4] For example, the content of the exploit is not released to the public at large. Only information about

---

[2] RFPolicy found on http://www.ilias.de/docu/goto_docu_wiki_1357_RFPolicy.html.

[3] Zero Day Initiative "Disclosure Policy" available at http://www.zerodayinitiative.com/advisories/disclosure_policy/.

[4] CERT/CC Vulnerability Disclosure Policy available at http://www.cert.org/kb/vul_disclosure.html.

vulnerabilities is released and even then, to a limited audience. Vulnerabilities are disclosed after 45 days.

Other responsible policies and codes of conduct contain similar provisions and may adopt different timeframes for disclosure and patching. Responsible disclosure policies seem to mimic some reoccurring themes:

- Contact the affected vendor and notify them of the vulnerability.
- Wait an appropriate time for vendor response to the problem.
- If vendor does not patch the problem within a specified time-frame, the vulnerability is disclosed.
- Disclosure may be full or partial.

Responsible disclosure policies are silent as regards to dealing with exploits in the marketplace—a practice which is plagued with ethical issues yet remains legal. Unfortunately, ethical and responsible disclosure by no means guarantees that a disclosure is legal. As we have seen in each of the Chapters, the legality of disclosures is not in question—it is illegal. Operating in this area, however, does not mean that one will get sued or face criminal charges. Much depends on prosecutorial will—there currently does not appear to be a strong will to pursue criminal charges and civil liability suits. The juxtaposition of what many perceive to be an extortionist yet legal exploit market with the possible legal risks faced by security researchers in exposing vulnerabilities and security risks, seems harsh and inappropriate.

I, along with countless others, have so far unsuccessfully argued that there should be a security research exemption to computer offences. Although this wish has not come to fruition, it hasn't stopped me from looking at different ways of tackling the problem.

If a security research exemption is adopted, special attention will need to be paid to the drafting of a security research exemption such that it is not open to abuse. One mechanism may be to adopt an approach where individuals and corporations in the security industry are required to be licensed.[5] This includes computer security entities. Only those licensed security entities would be entitled to use the security exemption. An additional feature would require security entities to report their activities pre-engagement of self-help mechanisms to a designated authority such as a CERT or its equivalent.

A complementary alternative is to provide a clear Code of Conduct for ethical engagement vulnerability disclosure. Where the entity strictly adhered to the Code of Conduct, they would be granted immunity against criminal and civil proceedings.

---

[5] [2].

References

1. McMillan R (2012) The Legacy of Linus Torvalds: Linux, Git, and One Giant Flamethrower. Available at http://www.wired.com/wiredenterprise/2012/11/linus-torvalds-isoc/all/M
2. Queensland Government Office of Fair Trading (2011) The various types of licenses and their requirements are available at http://www.fairtrading.qld.gov.au/security-industry-licence-types.htm (last accessed March 1)

Glossary of Terms

A **threat** is a circumstance that could result in harm, and may be natural, accidental or intentional. A party *directly* responsible for an intentional threat is referred to as an attacker.

Harm is anything that has deleterious consequences, and includes injury to persons, damage to property, financial loss, loss of value of an asset, and loss of reputation and confidence.

A **vulnerability** is a feature or weakness that gives rise to a susceptibility of a threat.

An **exploit** is an attack on a computer system that takes advantage of a vulnerability that the system offers to attackers. "Used as a verb, the term refers to the act of successfully making such an attack."[1]

A **safeguard** is a measure intended to avoid or reduce vulnerabilities.

A **known vulnerability** is a feature or weakness that has been made public through some form of communication, often publication.

A **zero day exploit** "is one that takes advantage of a security vulnerability on the same day that the vulnerability becomes generally known. There are zero days between the time the vulnerability is discovered and the first attack."[2]

A **future threat** is a circumstance that could result in harm as the result of a previously unknown security vulnerability.

Computer security is defined as a means ensuring the confidentiality, integrity, authentication and availability of information from threats to information which may include interception, interruption, modification, copying, fabrication, and deletion.

Botnet A botnet is a collection of compromised computers that are remotely controlled by a bot master.

---

[1] Rouse, foonote 5 in Chap. 1.

[2] Rouse, footnote 6 in Chap. 1.

A. Maurushat, *Disclosure of Security Vulnerabilities*, SpringerBriefs in Cybersecurity, DOI: 10.1007/978-1-4471-5004-6, © The Author(s) 2013

Compromised Computer The term "compromised computer"[3] is commonly used interchangeably, and in some cases wrongly, in the literature with "zombie", "bot" and "bot client", which confuses hardware with software, creates inconsistency of usage and may be confusing to users.[4] In this dissertation, a "compromised computer" is a computer that is connected to the Internet (an internet is a network that connects networks often using the protocols TCP/IP, and the Internet is the largest such internet)[5] and on which a bot is installed.[6] The computer is thus said to be compromised.

Bot A bot is software that is capable of being invoked from a remote location in order to provide the invoker with the capacity to cause the computer to perform a function.[7] Botnets have a modular structure whereby modules (bots) may be added or taken away from each bot to add new exploits and capabilities to it. This

---

[3] The term "compromised computer" has been selected over the term "compromised device". A computer may be as little as a processor, often a personal computer will contain multiple processors, or may be the world's largest computer. The term 'computer' is used here to refer to any computing device, even if is commonly called by some other name, and includes current and future devices with computing capabilities which may be connected to the Internet, including mobile phones, tablets, surveillance cameras, controllers for ADCs (analogue-digital converters) monitoring water-levels, etc. For this reason, Clarke, for example, prefers "device" (personal correspondence, Dr Roger Clarke). I have chosen "compromised computer", however, because it reflects the terminology used in computer science and information studies on botnets.

[4] The term 'zombie' has been appropriated by the computer security community as colloquial jargon for a compromised computer in a botnet. The reference of 'zombies' to botnets has been used humorously in writing on botnets:[4]

> In *The Night of the Living Dead*, zombies sucked brain matter in a frenzied hunger. In the computer world, a Trojan can be used to turn your PC into its own computing matter - turning it into a zombie machine. Once under the control of such an illicit program, the Trojan can be accessed by attackers intent on any number of ominous deeds.

[4] While the term 'zombie' is still used in association with botnets, the rhetoric among computer security experts has shifted from this humorous term to one which better connotes the serious problem of botnets. The term "bot" or "compromised computer" is replacing "zombie" in much of the botnet research and writing, including my own. My own personal reluctance to use the term "zombie" stems in part from my personal disdain for horror films and the monster genre but more importantly, from my experience in researching botnets and crime. I find it difficult to associate over-dramatised horror films and humour with a tool that is used to distribute child pornography, launch distributed denial of service attacks, steal personal information and perpetrate fraud, and to launch cyber warfare attacks, particularly if cyber warfare is followed by an actual war.

[5] TCP/IP is often used as a single acronym when in fact it references two key protocols. TCP refers to Transmission control protocol. TCP is a connection oriented protocol that establishes a communication channel known as a data stream between two network hosts. IP refers to internet protocol and is an addressing scheme that links to IP addresses. *See* Plfeeger [1].

[6] A computer may still be compromised in the absence of a botnet master. Where a controller is gone but where a botnet continues to infect computers, it is referred to as an "orphan botnet". *See* Gutman [2].

[7] Modified definition of Clarke's where he defines bots as "(Generally, a program that operates as an agent for a user or another program. More specifically) software that is capable of being invoked remotely in order to perform a particular function." Clarke [3].

ensures a botnet master's ability to rapidly respond to technical measures set up to infiltrate and take down the botnet.[8]

Bot-Server and Command and Control Source (C & C) Command and control refers to the communications infrastructure of a botnet. A botnet master issues commands and exercises control over the performance of bots. Bots fetch data from a pre-programmed location, and interpret that data as triggers for action, and instructions on what function to perform. The pre-programmed location is known as "the bot server" or "command and control" source. Command and Control is achieved by means of what is commonly called a 'bot-server'. The term 'server' refers to any software that provide services on request by another piece of software, which is called a client. The bot requests and the server responds. Where the client is a bot, the server is reasonably enough called a bot-server. Common bot servers are Internet Relay Chat (IRC) servers, HTTP-servers, the DNS (by means of TXT records), and peer-to-peer (P2P) nodes.

Traffic between the command and control source and its bots may be in clear or encrypted form. For example, IRC is an open network protocol which can also be used with Secure Sockets Layer (SSL). SSL enables the establishment of an encrypted channel. Where the command and control of a botnet occurs in IRC alone, the information is openly available for viewing and tracking. When SSL is used in conjunction with IRC, the information is encrypted and is, therefore, not visible to anyone who lacks access to the relevant decryption key. For the purpose of clarity, there will be no further reference to the term "bot server" unless found in a quote. Command and Control source (C and C) will be the term used throughout.

Botnet Master and Botnet Herder The term botnet master is used interchangeably in the literature with botnet herder and attacker.[9] In this dissertation, the terms are defined more precisely. A botnet herder refers to someone who both builds the botnet and then issues instructions to it. A botnet master, by contrast, is anyone who can distribute instruction to any given botnet, whether or not they were also the botnet herder. A botnet master uses any device convenient to them in order to make changes to the content on the bot-server that will be fetched by the bots.

Round Robin DNS involves the configuration of a domain to have several IP addresses. If any one IP address is blocked or ceases to be available, the others essentially back it up. Blocking or removing a single IP address, therefore, is not an effective solution to removing the content. The content merely rotates to another IP address.

Dynamic DNS is a service that enables the domain name entry for the relevant domain-name to be updated very promptly, every time the IP address changes. A dynamic DNS provider enablers a customer to either update the IP address via the provider's web page or using a tool that automatically detects the change in IP address and amends the DNS entry. To work effectively, the Time to Live (TTL) for the DNS entry must be set very short, to prevent cached entries scattered around the Internet serving up outdated IP-addresses. **FastFlux** is a particular dynamic DNS technique used by botnet masters whereby DNS records are

---

[8] Dunham [4].

[9] Provos, footnote 1 in Chap. 3.

frequently changed. This could be every 5 min.[10] Essentially, large volumes of IP addresses are rapidly rotated through the DNS records for a specific domain. This is similar to dynamic DNS tactics. The main difference between dynamic DNS and FastFlux is the automation and rapidity of rotation with a FastFlux botnet.[11] Some FastFlux botnets rotate IP addresses every 5 min, and others every hour.[12]

Multi-homing is a network that has multiple links from the Internet.

Distributed Command and Control (or Superbotnets) is a type of botnet that draws on a small botnet comprised of 15–20 bots. The botnet herders may have anywhere from 10,000 to 250,000 bots at their disposal, but use a select few for a particular purpose. The smaller botnet is then used to issue commands to larger botnets (hence the term distributed command and control).[13]

Encryption is the conversion of plain text into ciphertext. Encryption acts to conceal or prevent the meaning of the data from being known by parties without decryption codes. Botnet instructions commonly use encryption. Encrypted instruction can then not be analysed making investigating, mitigation and prevention much more difficult. Public key cryptography is often used. In public key cryptography, a twin pair of keys is created: one key is private, the other public. Their fundamental property is that, although one key cannot be derived from the other, a message encrypted by one key can only be decrypted by the other key.

Proxy servers refer to a service (a computer system or an application) that acts as an intermediary for requests from clients by forwarding requests to other servers. One use of proxy servers is to get around connection blocks such as authentication challenges and Internet filters. Another is to hide the origin of a connection. Proxy servers obfuscate a communication path such that User M connects to a website through proxy server B which again connects through proxy server Z whereby the packets appear to come from Z not M. Traceback, however to Z yields information of an additional hurdle as packets also appear to come from B. Other proxy servers such as Tor are anonymous. Tor is also known as an onion router. Tor is described as follows:

> Tor protects you by bouncing your communications around a distributed network of relays run by volunteers all around the world: it prevents somebody from watching your Internet connection from learning what sites you visit, and it prevents the sites you visit from learning your physical location.[14]

Tor is described as onion routing due to the use of multiple layers of proxy servers. This is similar to the multiple layers of an onion. Tor is used by users in heavily Internet-censored countries like China and Iran to access blocked websites

---

[10] *See* The Honeynet Organisation at http://www.honeynet.org/node/132 (last accessed February 6, 2011).

[11] Dunham [5].

[12] Gaaster [6].

[13] Barakat [7]. *See also* Vogt [8].

[14] Tor available at https://www.torproject.org. There are many other types of anonymising proxy servers and similar technologies such as Phantom Access Agent. See Zhao, X., Howe, D., Nissenbaum, H., and Mazeres, D., "Phantom Access Agent: a Client-Side Approach to Personal Information Control" available at http://www.nyu.edu/projects/nissenbaum/papers/paa.pdf.

as well as being used by some criminals to prevent law enforcement from trace-back to the source. Professional botnet masters, however, do not use Tor to obfuscate the origin as virtual private network services are more popular.[15]

Virtual Private Network Service (VPN) is a network that uses a public tele-communications infrastructure (usually the Internet) to connect remote sites or users together.[16] This connection allows a secure access to an organisation's network. Instead of a dedicated, real-world connection such as a leased line, a VPN uses "virtual" connections routed through the Internet from an organisation's private network to the remote site or employee."[17] VPN is made secure through cryptographic tunnelling protocols that provide confidentiality by blocking packet sniffing and interception software.

Rootkits are software or hardware devices designed to gain administrator-level control and sustain such control over a computer system without being detected.[18] A rootkit is used to obscure the operation of malware or a botnet from monitoring and investigation.

Peer-to-peer Communications (P2P) "is any distributed network architecture composed of participants that make a portion of their resources (such as processing power, disk storage or network bandwidth) directly available to other network participants, without the need for central coordination instances."[19] A P2P network relies on the capacity of multiple participants' computers, each of which has both client and server capabilities. This differs from conventional client-server architectures where a relatively low number of servers provide the core function of a service or application.[20] Such networks are useful for many purposes such as sharing of scientific information amongst researchers, file-sharing of videos and music, and for telephone traffic. P2P operates on peer nodes.[21] P2P may be used to send content in clear or encrypted format. The ad hoc distribution of P2P makes it an ideal bot server location for command and control. The use of P2P channels allows an additional layer of rapid IP address fluctuation.

Hacker "A person who delights in having an intimate understanding of the internal workings of a system, computers and computer networks in particular. The term is often misused in a pejorative context, where "cracker" would be the correct term."[22]

---

[15] Wouters [9].

[16] Virtual Private Network available at http://www.en.wikipedia.org/wiki/Virtual_private_network.

[17] Tyson, J., "How Virtual Private Networks Work" available at https://www.computer.howstuffworks.com/vpn.com.

[18] Pfleeger, footnote 1 in Chap. 2.

[19] The author looked any many different definitions of peer-to-peer and found the Wikipedia definition had the best description. *See* Wikipedia "Peer-to-peer" available at http://en.wikipedia.org/wiki/Peer-to-peer.

[20] *See generally*, Clarke [10].

[21] Oram [11].

[22] RFC 1392 Internet Users Glossary.

Cracker "A cracker is an individual who attempts to access computer systems without authorization. These individuals are often malicious, as opposed to hackers, and have many means at their disposal for breaking into a system."[23]

Black Hat Hacker (also referred to as a cracker), is "someone who uses his computer knowledge in criminal activities in order to obtain personal benefits. A typical example is a person who exploits the weaknesses of the systems of a financial institution for making some money."[24]

White Hat Hacker "Although white hat hacking can be considered similar to a black hacker, there is an important difference. A white hacker does it with no criminal intention in mind. Companies around the world, who want to test their systems, contract white hackers." [25] They will test the security of a system, and are often hired to make recommendations to improve such systems.

Grey Hat Hacker "A grey hat hacker is someone who is in between these two concepts. He may use his skills for legal or illegal acts, but not for personal gains. Grey hackers use their skills in order to prove themselves that they can accomplish a determined feat, but never do it in order to make money out of it. The moment they cross that boundary, they become black hat hackers."[26]

Hacktivism is the clever use of technology which involves unauthorised access to data or a computer system in pursuit of a cause or political ends."[27]

Online Civil Disobedience is the use of any technology that connects to the Internet in pursuit of a political ends.

Penetration/Intrusion Testing is a type of information systems security testing on behalf of the system's owners. This is known in the computer security world as "ethical hacking". There is some argument, however, as to whether penetration testing must be done with permission from a system's owners or whether a benevolent intention would suffice in the absence of permission. Whether permission is obtained or not obtained, however, does not change the common cause, that of improving security.

Security Activism is similar to penetration/intrusion testing in that the cause is to improve security. Security activism goes beyond mere testing of security, however, to gather intelligence on crackers, and to launch active attacks to disrupt criminal online enterprises. One example is the taking down of a botnet (see Sect. 7).

Counter-Attack is also referred to as hackback or strikeback. Counter-attack is when an individual or organisation who is subject to an attack on their data, network or computer takes similar measures to attack back at the "hacker/cracker". For example, when an individual or organisation is subject to a denial of service

---

[23] RFC 1392 Internet Users Glossary.

[24] Hacking Alert, "White Hat and Grey Hat Hacking: What is the Real Difference?" http://www.hackingalert.com/hacking-articles/grey-hat-hackers.php. *See also* Hafele 2004.

[25] Hacking Alert, "White Hat and Grey Hat Hacking: What is the Real Difference?" http://www.hackingalert.com/hacking-articles/grey-hat-hackers.php.

[26] Hacking Alert, "White Hat and Grey Hat Hacking: What is the Real Difference?" http://www.hackingalert.com/hacking-articles/grey-hat-hackers.php.

[27] Samuels [12].

attack, that organisation might initiate their own denial of service attack on the responsible party's website.

Ethical Hacking Ethical hacking then is the non-violent use of a technology in pursuit of a cause, political or otherwise which is often legally and morally ambiguous.[28]

Vulnerability is a feature or weakness that gives rise to a susceptibility to a threat. The term bug is used interchangeably with vulnerability in the context of computers. Computer bugs are problems or flaws with software or hardware.

Threat is a circumstance that could result in harm, and may be natural, accidental or intentional.

---

[28] Samuels, above.

Appendix A

A. Maurushat, *Disclosure of Security Vulnerabilities*, SpringerBriefs in Cybersecurity, DOI: 10.1007/978-1-4471-5004-6, © The Author(s) 2013

Table 1

	Convention	California and US Federal Law
Offences against the confidentiality, integrity and availability of computer data and systems	**Article 2 – Illegal access** Each Party shall adopt such legislative and other measures as may be necessary to establish as criminal offences under its domestic law, when committed intentionally, the access to the whole or any part of a computer system without right. A Party may require that the offence be committed by infringing security measures, with the intent of obtaining computer data or other dishonest intent, or in relation to a computer system that is connected to another computer system.	**California Penal Code s502 (c)(6)** knowingly and without permission providing a means to access any computer, computer sys, computer network **California Penal Code s502 (c)(7)** knowingly and without permission to access any computer, computer sys, computer network **Federal - 18 USC § 2701** Unlawful access to stored communications
	Article 3 – Illegal interception Each Party shall adopt such legislative and other measures as may be necessary to establish as criminal offences under its domestic law, when committed intentionally, the interception without right, made by technical means, of non-public transmissions of computer data to, from or within a computer system, including electromagnetic emissions from a computer system carrying such computer data. A Party may require that the offence be committed with dishonest intent, or in relation to a computer system that is connected to another computer system.	**Federal - 18 USC § 2511** Interception and disclosure of wire, oral or electronic communications prohibited
	Article 4 – Data interference 1. Each Party shall adopt such legislative and other measures as may be necessary to establish as criminal offences under its domestic law, when committed intentionally, the damaging, deletion, deterioration, alteration or suppression of computer data without right. 2. A Party may reserve the right to require that the conduct described in paragraph 1 result in serious harm.	**Federal - 18 USC § 2701** Unlawful access to stored communicationsIncludes the elements "obtains, alters, or prevents authorized access to a wire or electronic communication while it is in electronic storage" **California Penal Code s502 (c)(4)**knowingly and without permission adds, alters, damages, deletes, or destroys any data, computer software, or computer programs **California Penal Code s502 (c)(5)** knowingly and without permission disrupts or causes the disruption of computer services or denies or causes the denial of computer services to an authorised user **California Penal Code s502 (c)(8)** knowingly introduces any computer contaminant into any computer, computer sys or computer network

(continued)

Table 1 (continued)

Convention	California and US Federal Law
Article 5 – System interference Each Party shall adopt such legislative and other measures as may be necessary to establish as criminal offences under its domestic law, when committed intentionally, the serious hindering without right of the functioning of a computer system by inputing, transmitting, damaging, deleting, deteriorating, altering or suppressing computer data.	**Federal - 18 USC § 2512** Manufacture, distribution, possession, and advertising of wire, oral, or electronic communication intercepting devices prohibited **California Penal Code s502 (e)(2)** knowingly and without permission takes, copies, makes use of data from a computer, computer sys, or computer network **California Penal Code s502 (e)(3)** knowingly and without permission uses computer services
Article 6 – Misuse of devices 1. Each Party shall adopt such legislative and other measures as may be necessary to establish as criminal offences under its domestic law, when committed intentionally and without right: (a) the production, sale, procurement for use, import, distribution or otherwise making available of: (i) a device, including a computer program, designed or adapted primarily for the purpose of committing any of the offences established in accordance with Articles 2 through 5; (ii) a computer password, access code, or similar data by which the whole or any part of a computer system is capable of being accessed, with intent that it be used for the purpose of committing any of the offences established in Articles 2 through 5; and (b) the possession of an item referred to in paragraphs (a. i or ii) above, with intent that it be used for the purpose of committing any of the offences established in Articles 2 through 5. A Party may require by law that a number of such items be possessed before criminal liability attaches. 2. This article shall not be interpreted as imposing criminal liability where the production, sale, procurement for use, import, distribution or otherwise making available or possession referred to in paragraph 1 of this article is not for the purpose of committing an offence established in accordance with Articles 2 through 5 of this Convention, such as for the authorised testing or protection of a computer system. 3. Each Party may reserve the right not to apply paragraph 1 of this article, provided that the reservation does not concern the sale, distribution or otherwise making available of the items referred to in paragraph 1, a. ii of this article.	

(continued)

Table 1 (continued)

	Convention	California and US Federal Law
Forgery	**Article 7** Each Party shall adopt such legislative and other measures as may be necessary to establish as criminal offences under its domestic law, when committed intentionally and without right, the input, alteration, deletion, or suppression of computer data, resulting in inauthentic data with the intent that it be considered or acted upon for legal purposes as if it were authentic, regardless whether or not the data is directly readable and intelligible. A Party may require an intent to defraud, or similar dishonest intent, before criminal liability attaches.	**Federal - 18 USC § 474** Plates, stones, or analog, digital, or electronic images for counterfeiting obligations or securities **Federal - 18 USC § 476** Taking impressions of tools used for obligations or securities"impression" includes impression, stamp, analog, digital, or electronic image **Federal - 18 USC § 481** Plates, stones, or analog, digital, or electronic images for counterfeiting foreign obligations or securities **California Penal Code s502 (e)(9)** knowingly and without permission uses the Internet domain nameof another individual or corporationor entity to send out emails and thereby damages or causes damages to a computer, computer sys or computer network **California Penal Code s480** in possession of any apparatus in counterfeiting gold dust, gold or silver bars, bullion, lumps, pieces, or nuggets, or in counterfeiting bank notes or bills. 'apparatus' = includes computer, computer sys or computer network pursuant to s502. **California Penal Code s483.5** no deceptive identification document (eg driver's license or social security card) by document-making device'document-making device' = computer file, computer disk, electronic device, hologram, laminate machine or computer hardware or software, etc **California Penal Code s530.5** wilfully obtains personal identifying info and uses it for unlawful purpose

(continued)

Table 1 (continued)

	Convention	California and US Federal Law
Online Fraud	**Article 8** Each Party shall adopt such legislative and other measures as may be necessary to establish as criminal offences under its domestic law, when committed intentionally and without right, the causing of a loss of property to another person by: (a) any input, alteration, deletion or suppression of computer data, (b) any interference with the functioning of a computer system, with fraudulent or dishonest intent of procuring, without right, an economic benefit for oneself or for another person.	**Federal - 18 USC § 1030** Fraud and related activity in connection with computers This includes credit card/bank account fraud (subsection (2)) **Federal - 18 USC § 1343** Fraud by wire, radio, or television **California Penal Code s530** Identity theft law **California Penal Code s484e** Credit card fraud law **California Penal Code s502 (c)(1)** access and without permission access computer data to defraud or wrongfully control or obtain money, property or data
Child Sexual Exploitation Materials	**Article 9** 1. Each Party shall adopt such legislative and other measures as may be necessary to establish as criminal offences under its domestic law, when committed intentionally and without right, the following conduct: (a)producing child pornography for the purpose of its distribution through a computer system; (b) offering or making available child pornography through a computer system; (c) distributing or transmitting child pornography through a computer system; (d) procuring child pornography through a computer system for oneself or for another person; (e) possessing child pornography in a computer system or on a computer-data storage medium.2. For the purpose of paragraph 1 above, the term "child pornography" shall include pornographic material that visually depicts: (a) a minor engaged in sexually explicit conduct; (b) a person appearing to be a minor engaged in sexually explicit conduct; (c) realistic images representing a minor engaged in sexually explicit conduct. 3. For the purpose of paragraph 2 above, the term "minor" shall include all persons under 18 years of age. A Party may, however, require a lower age-limit, which shall be not less than 16 years. 4. Each Party may reserve the right not to apply, in whole or in part, paragraphs 1, sub-paragraphs d. and e, and 2, sub-paragraphs b. and c.	**Federal - 18 USC § 1466A** Obscene visual representations of the sexual abuse of children Communication by computer is a circumstance included in (d). The definition of "visual depiction" includes "undeveloped film and videotape, and data stored on a computer disk or by electronic means which is capable of conversion into a visual image, and also includes any … digital image or picture, computer image or picture, or computer generated image or picture, whether made or produced by electronic, mechanical, or other means" **Federal - 18 USC § 2252** Certain activities relating to material involving the sexual exploitation of minors & **18 USC § 2252A** Certain activities relating to material constituting or containing child pornography All active terms include those actions done by computer, e.g. distributes or accesses by computer. **California Penal Code s311**knowingly sends or distribute or in this State possesses, publishes, develops info, data or image, any film, computer hardware & software, floppy disc, data storage medium, CD-ROM to mention a few, child sexual exploitation materials

(continued)

Table 1 (continued)

	Convention	California and US Federal Law
Copyright Infringement Crimes	**Article 10** 1. Each Party shall adopt such legislative and other measures as may be necessary to establish as criminal offences under its domestic law the infringement of copyright, as defined under the law of that Party, pursuant to the obligations it has undertaken under the Paris Act of 24 July 1971 revising the Bern Convention for the Protection of Literary and Artistic Works, the Agreement on Trade-Related Aspects of Intellectual Property Rights and the WIPO Copyright Treaty, with the exception of any moral rights conferred by such conventions, where such acts are committed wilfully, on a commercial scale and by means of a computer system. 2. Each Party shall adopt such legislative and other measures as may be necessary to establish as criminal offences under its domestic law the infringement of related rights, as defined under the law of that Party, pursuant to the obligations it has undertaken under the International Convention for the Protection of Performers, Producers of Phonograms and Broadcasting Organisations (Rome Convention), the Agreement on Trade-Related Aspects of Intellectual Property Rights and the WIPO Performances and Phonograms Treaty, with the exception of any moral rights conferred by such conventions, where such acts are committed wilfully, on a commercial scale and by means of a computer system. 3. A Party may reserve the right not to impose criminal liability under paragraphs 1 and 2 of this article in limited circumstances, provided that other effective remedies are available and that such reservation does not derogate from the Party's international obligations set forth in the international instruments referred to in paragraphs 1 and 2 of this article.	**Federal - 18 USC § 2319** Criminal infringement of a copyright **Federal - The No Electronic Theft Act (NET Act)** federal crime to reproduce, distribute, or share copies of electronic copyrighted workson the Internet even if there is no commercial purpose nor financial gain

(continued)

Table 1 (continued)

	Convention	California and US Federal Law
ADDITIONAL PROTOCOL TO THE CONVENTION ON CYBERCRIME		
Online Harassing	**Article 3 – Dissemination of racist and xenophobic material through computer systems**	**Federal - 18 USC § 2261A** Stalking
	1. Each Party shall adopt such legislative and other measures as may be necessary to establish as criminal offences under its domestic law, when committed intentionally and without right, the following conduct: distributing, or otherwise making available, racist and xenophobic material to the public through a computer system.	Includes the elements "uses … any interactive computer service, … to engage in a course of conduct that causes substantial emotional distress to that person or places that person in reasonable fear of the death of, or serious bodily injury."
	2. A Party may reserve the right not to attach criminal liability to conduct as defined by paragraph 1 of this article, where the material, as defined in Article 2, paragraph 1, advocates, promotes or incites discrimination that is not associated with hatred or violence, provided that other effective remedies are available.	**Federal - 18 USC § 876** Mailing threatening communications **California Penal Code s1708.7** pattern of conduct of harassing, causing fear for safety with credible threat 'credible threat' = verbal/written threat including communicated by means of an electronic communication device, eg, not limited to cellular telephones, computers, etc.
	3. Notwithstanding paragraph 2 of this article, a Party may reserve the right not to apply paragraph 1 to those cases of discrimination for which, due to established principles in its national legal system concerning freedom of expression, it cannot provide for effective remedies as referred to in the said paragraph 2.	**California Penal Code s422** wilfully threatens to commit a crime with intent in writing or verbally or by means of electronic communication device is to be taken as a threat. 'electronic communication device' = not limited to cellular telephones, computers, etc
		California Penal Code s646.9 willfully, maliciously, and repeatedly follows or willfully and maliciously harasses another person and who makes a credible threat with the intent to place that person in reasonable fear for his or her safety, or the safety of his or her immediate family 'electronic communication device' = not limited to cellular telephones, computers, etc
		California Penal Code s653.2 intent to place another person in reasonable fear for his or her safety, or the safety of the other person's immediate family, by means of an electronic communication device Harassment by electronically distributes, publishes, e-mails, hyperlinks, or makes available for downloading, personal identifying information, including, but not limited to, a digital image of another person, or an electronic message of a harassing nature about another person

(continued)

Table 1 (continued)

	Convention	California and US Federal Law
Hate Speech	**Article 4 – Racist and xenophobic motivated threat**	**Federal - 18 USC § 1461**
	1. Each Party shall adopt such legislative and other measures as may be necessary to establish as criminal offences under its domestic law, when committed intentionally and without right, the following conduct: threatening, through a computer system, with the commission of a serious criminal offence as defined under its domestic law, (i) persons for the reason that they belong to a group, distinguished by race, colour, descent or national or ethnic origin, as well as religion, if used as a pretext for any of these factors, or (ii) a group of persons which is distinguished by any of these characteristics.	Mailing obscene or crime-inciting matter This provision is mostly targeted to materials promoting abortion, but does include the definition: "The term "indecent", as used in this section includes matter of a character tending to incite arson, murder, or assassination." **California Penal Code s422.6(c)** high threshold test of showing that that the speech itself threatened violence against a specific person or group of persons and that the defendant had the apparent ability to carry out the threat - free speech protection
Criminal Defamation	Article 5 – Racist and xenophobic motivated insult	**California Civil Code s44-48**
	1. Each Party shall adopt such legislative and other measures as may be necessary to establish as criminal offences under its domestic law, when committed intentionally and without right, the following conduct: insulting publicly, through a computer system, (i) persons for the reason that they belong to a group distinguished by race, colour, descent or national or ethnic origin, as well as religion, if used as a pretext for any of these factors; or (ii) a group of persons which is distinguished by any of these characteristics. 2. A Party may either: (a) require that the offence referred to in paragraph 1 of this article has the effect that the person or group of persons referred to in paragraph 1 is exposed to hatred, contempt or ridicule; or (b) reserve the right not to apply, in whole or in part, paragraph 1 of this article.	Californian defamation laws. **Protection of s230 of the Communications Decency Act**Protection for online ISPs and users from actions against them based on contents of 3rd parties - immunises both ISPs and Internet users from liability for torts committed by others using their website or online forum, even if the provider fails to take action after receiving actual notice of the harmful or offensive content

(continued)

Table 1 (continued)

	Convention	California and US Federal Law
Denial, gross minimisation, approval or justification of genocide or crimes against humanity	**Article 6 – Denial, gross minimisation, approval or justification of genocide or crimes against humanity** 1. Each Party shall adopt such legislative measures as may be necessary to establish the following conduct as criminal offences under its domestic law, when committed intentionally and without right: distributing or otherwise making available, through a computer system to the public, material which denies, grossly minimises, approves or justifies acts constituting genocide or crimes against humanity, as defined by international law and recognised as such by final and binding decisions of the International Military Tribunal, established by the London Agreement of 8 August 1945, or of any other international court established by relevant international instruments and whose jurisdiction is recognised by that Party. 2. A Party may either (a) require that the denial or the gross minimisation referred to in paragraph 1 of this article is committed with the intent to incite hatred, discrimination or violence against any individual or group of individuals, based on race, colour, descent or national or ethnic origin, as well as religion if used as a pretext for any of these factors, or otherwise (b) reserve the right not to apply, in whole or in part, paragraph 1 of this article.	**Federal - 18 USC § 1091** Genocide (c) Incitement Offence **NONE FOUND IN CALIFORNIAN STATE LEGISLATION**

Table 2

	Convention	Canada
Offences against the confidentiality, integrity and availability of computer data and systems	**Article 2 – Illegal access** Each Party shall adopt such legislative and other measures as may be necessary to establish as criminal offences under its domestic law, when committed intentionally, the access to the whole or any part of a computer system without right. A Party may require that the offence be committed by infringing security measures, with the intent of obtaining computer data or other dishonest intent, or in relation to a computer system that is connected to another computer system.	**Section 342.1 of the Criminal Code** Unauthorised use of computer to commit an offence in relation to Section 430.
	Article 3 – Illegal interception Each Party shall adopt such legislative and other measures as may be necessary to establish as criminal offences under its domestic law, when committed intentionally, the interception without right, made by technical means, of non-public transmissions of computer data to, from or within a computer system, including electromagnetic emissions from a computer system carrying such computer data. A Party may require that the offence be committed with dishonest intent, or in relation to a computer system that is connected to another computer system.	Computer System = a device that, or a group of interconnected or related devices one or more of which, (a) contains computer programs or other data, and (b) pursuant to computer programs, (i) performs logic and control, and (ii) may perform any other function Data = representations of information or of concepts that are being prepared or have been prepared in a form suitable for use in a computer system
	Article 4 – Data interference 1. Each Party shall adopt such legislative and other measures as may be necessary to establish as criminal offences under its domestic law, when committed intentionally, the damaging, deletion, deterioration, alteration or suppression of computer data without right. 2. A Party may reserve the right to require that the conduct described in paragraph 1 result in serious harm.	**Section 430 (1.1) of the Criminal Code** Commits mischief which amounts to an indictable offence for the wilful destroying, altering or interferes with the lawful use of data
	Article 5 – System interference Each Party shall adopt such legislative and other measures as may be necessary to establish as criminal offences under its domestic law, when committed intentionally, the serious hindering without right of the functioning of a computer system by inputting, transmitting, damaging, deleting, deteriorating, altering or suppressing computer data.	

(continued)

Table 2 (continued)

Convention	Canada
Article 6 – Misuse of devices 1. Each Party shall adopt such legislative and other measures as may be necessary to establish as criminal offences under its domestic law, when committed intentionally and without right:	**Section 326 (1)(b) of the Criminal Code** Commits theft who fradulently, maliciously or without a colour of right uses any telecommunication facility or obtains any telecommunication services
(a) the production, sale, procurement for use, import, distribution or otherwise making available of: (i) a device, including a computer program, designed or adapted primarily for the purpose of committing any of the offences established in accordance with Articles 2 through 5;	**Section 327 (1) of the Criminal Code** Without lawful excuse, the proof of which lies on him, manufactures, possesses, sells or offers for sale or distributes any instrument or device or any component thereof, the design of which renders it
(ii) a computer password, access code, or similar data by which the whole or any part of a computer system is capable of being accessed, with intent that it be used for the purpose of committing any of the offences established in Articles 2 through 5; and	primarily useful for obtaining the use of any telecommunication facility or service, under circumstances that give rise to a reasonable inference that the device has been used or is or was intended to be used to obtain the use of any telecommunication
(b) the possession of an item referred to in paragraphs a.i or ii above, with intent that it be used for the purpose of committing any of the offences established in Articles 2 through 5. A Party may require by law that a number of such items be possessed before criminal liability attaches.	facility or service without payment of a lawful charge therefor, is guilty of an indictable offence.
2. This article shall not be interpreted as imposing criminal liability where the production, sale, procurement for use, import, distribution or otherwise making available or possession referred to in paragraph 1 of this article is not for the purpose of committing an offence established in accordance with Articles 2 through 5 of this Convention, such as for the authorised testing or protection of a computer system.	
3. Each Party may reserve the right not to apply paragraph 1 of this article, provided that the reservation does not concern the sale, distribution or otherwise making available of the items referred to in paragraph 1, a, ii of this article.	
Article 7 Each Party shall adopt such legislative and other measures as may be necessary to establish as criminal offences under its domestic law, when committed intentionally and without right, the input, alteration, deletion, or suppression of computer data, resulting in inauthentic data with the intent that it be considered or acted upon for legal purposes as if it were authentic, regardless whether or not the data is directly readable and intelligible. A Party may require an intent to defraud, or similar dishonest intent, before criminal liability attaches.	**Section 366 of the Criminal Code** Deals largely with forgery and offences resembling forgery. However, there are no provision for forgery committed by the way of alteration of computer data resulting in inauthentic data with intent to be considered or acted upon as if it were authentic.

Forgery (row label for Article 7)

(continued)

Table 2 (continued)

	Convention	Canada
Online Fraud	**Article 8** Each Party shall adopt such legislative and other measures as may be necessary to establish as criminal offences under its domestic law, when committed intentionally and without right, the causing of a loss of property to another person by: (a) any input, alteration, deletion or suppression of computer data, (b) any interference with the functioning of a computer system, with fraudulent or dishonest intent of procuring, without right, an economic benefit for oneself or for another person.	**Part X of the Criminal Code** Deals largely with fraud and related fraudulent conduct. However, there are no provision for fraud committed of computer data using a computer system.
Child Sexual Exploitation Materials	**Article 9** 1. Each Party shall adopt such legislative and other measures as may be necessary to establish as criminal offences under its domestic law, when committed intentionally and without right, the following conduct: (a) producing child pornography for the purpose of its distribution through a computer system; (b) offering or making available child pornography through a computer system;(c) distributing or transmitting child pornography through a computer system; (d) procuring child pornography through a computer system for oneself or for another person;e)possessing child pornography in a computer system or on a computer-data storage medium. 2. For the purpose of paragraph 1 above, the term "child pornography" shall include pornographic material that visually depicts: (a) a minor engaged in sexually explicit conduct; (b) a person appearing to be a minor engaged in sexually explicit conduct; (c) realistic images representing a minor engaged in sexually explicit conduct.3. For the purpose of paragraph 2 above, the term "minor" shall include all persons under 18 years of age. A Party may, however, require a lower age-limit, which shall be not less than 16 years. 4. Each Party may reserve the right not to apply, in whole or in part, paragraphs 1, sub-paragraphs d. and e, and 2. sub-paragraphs b. and c.	**Section 163.1 of the Criminal Code** Subsection 1 – Definition Similar to Clause 2, 3 & 4 in corresponding Article Subsection 2 - Making child pornography No indication of said offence depicting production of child pornography for the purpose of its distribution through a computer system Subsection 3 - Distribution Distribution of any child pornography guilty of an indictable offence punishable on summary convictions. No indication of said offence depicting offering or make available or distribute or transmit or procure of child pornography through a computer system Subsection 4 – Possession No indication of said offence depicting possession of child pornography in a computer system or on a computer-data storage medium **An Act respecting the mandatory reporting of Internet child pornography by persons who provide an Internet service, SC 2011, c 4** Act that requires mandatory report of Internet child pornogrpahy activities by Internet providers Corresponding Regulation: **Internet Child Pornography Reporting Regulations, SOR/2011-292**

(continued)

Table 2 (continued)

	Convention	Canada
	Article 10	**Bill C-11 before 41st Parliament, assented 29 Jun 2012**
Copyright Infringement Crimes	1. Each Party shall adopt such legislative and other measures as may be necessary to establish as criminal offences under its domestic law the infringement of copyright, as defined under the law of that Party, pursuant to the obligations it has undertaken under the Paris Act of 24 July 1971 revising the Bern Convention for the Protection of Literary and Artistic Works, the Agreement on Trade-Related Aspects of Intellectual Property Rights and the WIPO Copyright Treaty, with the exception of any moral rights conferred by such conventions, where such acts are committed wilfully, on a commercial scale and by means of a computer system.	Bill is submitted to specifically deal with copyright in the digital era and complies with the WIPO internet treaties
	2. Each Party shall adopt such legislative and other measures as may be necessary to establish as criminal offences under its domestic law the infringement of related rights, as defined under the law of that Party, pursuant to the obligations it has undertaken under the International Convention for the Protection of Performers, Producers of Phonograms and Broadcasting Organisations (Rome Convention), the Agreement on Trade-Related Aspects of Intellectual Property Rights and the WIPO Performances and Phonograms Treaty, with the exception of any moral rights conferred by such conventions, where such acts are committed wilfully, on a commercial scale and by means of a computer system.	Clauses 9 & 10 - new right for performers to make a sound recording available over the internet, pursuant to two 1996 WIPO Internet Treaties. Clauses 47-49 - techonological protection measures
	3. A Party may reserve the right not to impose criminal liability under paragraphs 1 and 2 of this article in limited circumstances, provided that other effective remedies are available and that such reservation does not derogate from the Party's international obligations set forth in the international instruments referred to in paragraphs 1 and 2 of this article.	

(continued)

Table 2 (continued)

	Convention	Canada
ADDITIONAL PROTOCOL TO THE CONVENTION ON CYBERCRIME		
Online Harassing	Article 3 – Dissemination of racist and xenophobic material through computer systems 1. Each Party shall adopt such legislative and other measures as may be necessary to establish as criminal offences under its domestic law, when committed intentionally and without right, the following conduct: distributing, or otherwise making available, racist and xenophobic material to the public through a computer system. 2. A Party may reserve the right not to attach criminal liability to conduct as defined by paragraph 1 of this article, where the material, as defined in Article 2, paragraph 1, advocates, promotes or incites discrimination that is not associated with hatred or violence, provided that other effective remedies are available. 3. Notwithstanding paragraph 2 of this article, a Party may reserve the right not to apply paragraph 1 to those cases of discrimination for which, due to established principles in its national legal system concerning freedom of expression, it cannot provide for effective remedies as referred to in the said paragraph 2.	**Bill C-273 before 41st Parliament, now 2nd Reading and Referral to Committee in the House of Commons** Clause 1 - addition to Section 264 subsection (2) of the Criminal Code to allow for conduct communicated by a computer and a group of interconnected or related computers including the Internet Clause 3 - addition to Section 372 subsection (3) of the Criminal Code to allow for sending repeated electronic messages an offence punishable on summary conviction
Hate Speech	Article 4 – Racist and xenophobic motivated threat 1. Each Party shall adopt such legislative and other measures as may be necessary to establish as criminal offences under its domestic law, when committed intentionally and without right, the following conduct: threatening, through a computer system, with the commission of a serious criminal offence as defined under its domestic law, (i) persons for the reason that they belong to a group, distinguished by race, colour, descent or national or ethnic origin, as well as religion, if used as a pretext for any of these factors, or (ii) a group of persons which is distinguished by any of these characteristics.	**Bill C-273 before 41st Parliament, now 2nd Reading and Referral to Committee in the House of Commons** Clause 3 - replacement of Section 372 subsection (1) of the Criminal Code to allow for communication by a computer and a group of interconnected or related computers including the Internet Clause 3 - addition of subsection (2) of the criminal code to allow for the sending of indecent electronic message an offence punishable by summary conviction

(continued)

Table 2 (continued)

	Convention	Canada
Copyright Infringement Crimes	**Article 10** 1. Each Party shall adopt such legislative and other measures as may be necessary to establish as criminal offences under its domestic law the infringement of copyright, as defined under the law of that Party, pursuant to the obligations it has undertaken under the Paris Act of 24 July 1971 revising the Bern Convention for the Protection of Literary and Artistic Works, the Agreement on Trade-Related Aspects of Intellectual Property Rights and the WIPO Copyright Treaty, with the exception of any moral rights conferred by such conventions, where such acts are committed wilfully, on a commercial scale and by means of a computer system. 2. Each Party shall adopt such legislative and other measures as may be necessary to establish as criminal offences under its domestic law the infringement of related rights, as defined under the law of that Party, pursuant to the obligations it has undertaken under the International Convention for the Protection of Performers, Producers of Phonograms and Broadcasting Organisations (Rome Convention), the Agreement on Trade-Related Aspects of Intellectual Property Rights and the WIPO Performances and Phonograms Treaty, with the exception of any moral rights conferred by such conventions, where such acts are committed wilfully, on a commercial scale and by means of a computer system. 3. A Party may reserve the right not to impose criminal liability under paragraphs 1 and 2 of this article in limited circumstances, provided that other effective remedies are available and that such reservation does not derogate from the Party's international obligations set forth in the international instruments referred to in paragraphs 1 and 2 of this article.	**Bill C-11 before 41st Parliament, assented 29 Jun 2012** Bill is submitted to specifically deal with copyright in the digital era and complies with the WIPO internet treaties Clauses 9 & 10 - new right for performers to make a sound recording available over the internet, pursuant to two 1996 WIPO Internet Treaties. Clauses 47-49 - techonological protection measures

(continued)

Table 2 (continued)

	Convention	Canada

ADDITIONAL PROTOCOL TO THE CONVENTION ON CYBERCRIME

Online Harassing

Convention:

Article 3 – Dissemination of racist and xenophobic material through computer systems

1. Each Party shall adopt such legislative and other measures as may be necessary to establish as criminal offences under its domestic law, when committed intentionally and without right, the following conduct: distributing, or otherwise making available, racist and xenophobic material to the public through a computer system.

2. A Party may reserve the right not to attach criminal liability to conduct as defined by paragraph 1 of this article, where the material, as defined in Article 2, paragraph 1, advocates, promotes or incites discrimination that is not associated with hatred or violence, provided that other effective remedies are available.

3. Notwithstanding paragraph 2 of this article, a Party may reserve the right not to apply paragraph 1 to those cases of discrimination for which, due to established principles in its national legal system concerning freedom of expression, it cannot provide for effective remedies as referred to in the said paragraph 2.

Canada:

Bill C-273 before 41st Parliament, now 2nd Reading and Referral to Committee in the House of Commons

Clause 1 - addition to Section 264 subsection (2) of the Criminal Code to allow for conduct communicated by a computer and a group of interconnected or related computers including the Internet

Clause 3 - addition to Section 372 subsection (3) of the Criminal Code to allow for sending repeated electronic messages an offence punishable on summary conviction

Hate Speech

Convention:

Article 4 – Racist and xenophobic motivated threat

1. Each Party shall adopt such legislative and other measures as may be necessary to establish as criminal offences under its domestic law, when committed intentionally and without right, the following conduct: threatening, through a computer system, with the commission of a serious criminal offence as defined under its domestic law, (i) persons for the reason that they belong to a group, distinguished by race, colour, descent or national or ethnic origin, as well as religion, if used as a pretext for any of these factors, or (ii) a group of persons which is distinguished by any of these characteristics.

Canada:

Bill C-273 before 41st Parliament, now 2nd Reading and Referral to Committee in the House of Commons

Clause 3 - replacement of Section 372 subsection (1) of the Criminal Code to allow for communication by a computer and a group of interconnected or related computers including the Internet

Clause 3 - addition of subsection (2) of the criminal code to allow for the sending of indecent electronic message an offence punishable by summary conviction

(continued)

Table 2 (continued)

	Convention	Canada
Criminal Defamation	Article 5 – Racist and xenophobic motivated insult 1. Each Party shall adopt such legislative and other measures as may be necessary to establish as criminal offences under its domestic law, when committed intentionally and without right, the following conduct: insulting publicly, through a computer system, (i) persons for the reason that they belong to a group distinguished by race, colour, descent or national or ethnic origin, as well as religion, if used as a pretext for any of these factors; or (ii) a group of persons which is distinguished by any of these characteristics. 2. A Party may either: (a) require that the offence referred to in paragraph 1 of this article has the effect that the person or group of persons referred to in paragraph 1 is exposed to hatred, contempt or ridicule; or (b) reserve the right not to apply, in whole or in part, paragraph 1 of this article.	**Bill C-273 before 41st Parliament, now 2nd Reading and Referral to Committee in the House of Commons** Clause 2 - addition to Section 298 subsection (2) of the Criminal Code to allow for publication by a computer and a group of interconnected or related computers including the Internet
Denial, gross minimisation, approval or justification of genocide or crimes against humanity	**Article 6 – Denial, gross minimisation, approval or justification of genocide or crimes against humanity** 1. Each Party shall adopt such legislative measures as may be necessary to establish the following conduct as criminal offences under its domestic law, when committed intentionally and without right: distributing or otherwise making available, through a computer system to the public, material which denies, grossly minimises, approves or justifies acts constituting genocide or crimes against humanity, as defined by international law and recognised as such by final and binding decisions of the International Military Tribunal, established by the London Agreement of 8 August 1945, or of any other international court established by relevant international instruments and whose jurisdiction is recognised by that Party. 2. A Party may either(a) require that the denial or the gross minimisation referred to in paragraph 1 of this article is committed with the intent to incite hatred, discrimination or violence against any individual or group of individuals, based on race, colour, descent or national or ethnic origin, as well as religion if used as a pretext for any of these factors, or otherwise (b) reserve the right not to apply, in whole or in part, paragraph 1 of this article.	NO KNOWN LEGISLATION IS SIMILIAR TO / COMPLIES WITH THIS ARTICLE

Table 3

	Convention	Hong Kong
Offences against the confidentiality, integrity and availability of computer data and systems	**Article 2 – Illegal access** Each Party shall adopt such legislative and other measures as may be necessary to establish as criminal offences under its domestic law, when committed intentionally, the access to the whole or any part of a computer system without right. A Party may require that the offence be committed by infringing security measures, with the intent of obtaining computer data or other dishonest intent, or in relation to a computer system that is connected to another computer system. **Article 3 – Illegal interception** Each Party shall adopt such legislative and other measures as may be necessary to establish as criminal offences under its domestic law, when committed intentionally, the interception without right, made by technical means, of non-public transmissions of computer data to, from or within a computer system, including electromagnetic emissions from a computer system carrying such computer data. A Party may require that the offence be committed with dishonest intent, or in relation to a computer system that is connected to another computer system. **Article 4 – Data interference** 1. Each Party shall adopt such legislative and other measures as may be necessary to establish as criminal offences under its domestic law, when committed intentionally, the damaging, deletion, deterioration, alteration or suppression of computer data without right. 2. A Party may reserve the right to require that the conduct described in paragraph 1 result in serious harm.	**Telecommunication Ordinance Cap.106** S27A – Unauthorised access to computer by telecommunications S2 – "telecommunication" = any transmission, emission or reception of communication by means of guided or unguided electromagnetic energy or both, other than any transmission or emission intended to be received or perceived directly by the human eye **Interception of Communication Ordinance Cap.532** S3 – a person who intentionally intercepts a communication in the course of its transmission by post or by means of telecommunication system shall be guilty of an offence S9 – a person who intentionally discloses to any other person any intercepted material is an offence **Crimes Ordinance Cap. 200**S60 (1) – destroying or damaging property S59(1)(b) – "property" = any program, or data, held in a computer or in a computer storage medium, whether or not the program or data is property of a tangible nature S59 (1A) – "destroy or damage" = misuse of a computer: • to cause a computer to function other than as it has been established to function by or on behalf of its owner, notwithstanding that the misuse may not impair the operation of the computer or a program held in the computer or the reliability of data held in the computer; • to alter or erase any program or data held in a computer or in a computer storage medium; • to add any program or data to the contents of a computer or of a computer storage medium.

(continued)

Table 3 (continued)

Convention	Hong Kong
Article 5 – System interference Each Party shall adopt such legislative and other measures as may be necessary to establish as criminal offences under its domestic law, when committed intentionally, the serious hindering without right of the functioning of a computer system by inputting, transmitting, damaging, deleting, deteriorating, altering or suppressing computer data.	**Crimes Ordinance Cap. 200** S60 (1) – destroying or damaging property S59(1)(b) – "property" = any program, or data, held in a computer or in a computer storage medium, whether or not the program or data is property of a tangible nature S59 (1A) – "destroy or damage" = misuse of a computer:• to cause a computer to function other than as it has been established to function by or on behalf of its owner, notwithstanding that the misuse may not impair the operation of the computer or a program held in the computer or the reliability of data held in the computer; • to alter or erase any program or data held in a computer or in a computer storage medium; • to add any program or data to the contents of a computer or of a computer storage medium. S161 – access to computer with criminal /dishonest intents 161(2) – "gain" or "loss" = gain or loss in money or other property, temporary or permanent

Article 6 – Misuse of devices 1. Each Party shall adopt such legislative and other measures as may be necessary to establish as criminal offences under its domestic law, when committed intentionally and without right:
(a) the production, sale, procurement for use, import, distribution or otherwise making available of:
(i) a device, including a computer program, designed or adapted primarily for the purpose of committing any of the offences established in accordance with Articles 2 through 5;
(ii) a computer password, access code, or similar data by which the whole or any part of a computer system is capable of being accessed, with intent that it be used for the purpose of committing any of the offences established in Articles 2 through 5; and
(b) the possession of an item referred to in paragraphs (a, i or ii) above, with intent that it be used for the purpose of committing any of the offences established in Articles 2 through 5. A Party may require by law that a number of such items be possessed before criminal liability attaches.
2. This article shall not be interpreted as imposing criminal liability where the production, sale, procurement for use, import, distribution or otherwise making available or possession referred to in paragraph 1 of this article is not for the purpose of committing an offence established in accordance with Articles 2 through 5 of this Convention, such as for the authorised testing or protection of a computer system.
3. Each Party may reserve the right not to apply paragraph 1 of this article, provided that the reservation does not concern the sale, distribution or otherwise making available of the items referred to in paragraph 1, a, ii of this article.

(continued)

Table 3 (continued)

	Convention	Hong Kong
Forgery	**Article 7** Each Party shall adopt such legislative and other measures as may be necessary to establish as criminal offences under its domestic law, when committed intentionally and without right, the input, alteration, deletion, or suppression of computer data, resulting in inauthentic data with the intent that it be considered or acted upon for legal purposes as if it were authentic, regardless whether or not the data is directly readable and intelligible. A Party may require an intent to defraud, or similar dishonest intent, before criminal liability attaches.	**Crime Ordinance, Cap. 200** S85 – making false entry in bank books85(2) – "book" = includes any disc, card, tape, microchip, sound track, or other device on or in which information is stored by mechanical, electronic , optical or other means **Theft Ordinance, Cap. 210** S19 - extending the meaning of false accounting to include destroying, defacing, concealing or falsifying records kept by computer S19 (2) – False Accounting S19 (3) – record includes record kept by the means of computer
Online Fraud	**Article 8** Each Party shall adopt such legislative and other measures as may be necessary to establish as criminal offences under its domestic law, when committed intentionally and without right, the causing of a loss of property to another person by: (a) any input, alteration, deletion or suppression of computer data, (b) any interference with the functioning of a computer system, with fraudulent or dishonest intent of procuring, without right, an economic benefit for oneself or for another person.	**Theft Ordinance, Cap. 210** S11 - extending the meaning of burglary to include unlawfully causing a computer to function other than as it has been established and altering, erasing or adding any computer program or data S11 (3A) – burglary including: • unlawfully causing a computer in the building to function other than as it has been established • unlawfully altering or erasing any program, or data, held in a computer in the building or in a computer storage medium in the building; and • unlawfully adding any program or data to the contents of a computer in the building or a computer storage medium in the building.

(continued)

Table 3 (continued)

	Convention	Hong Kong
Child Sexual Exploitation Materials	**Article 9** 1. Each Party shall adopt such legislative and other measures as may be necessary to establish as criminal offences under its domestic law, when committed intentionally and without right, the following conduct: (a) producing child pornography for the purpose of its distribution through a computer system; (b) offering or making available child pornography through a computer system; (c) distributing or transmitting child pornography through a computer system; (d) procuring child pornography through a computer system for oneself or for another person; (e) possessing child pornography in a computer system or on a computer-data storage medium. 2. For the purpose of paragraph 1 above, the term "child pornography" shall include pornographic material that visually depicts: (a) a minor engaged in sexually explicit conduct; (b) a person appearing to be a minor engaged in sexually explicit conduct; (c) realistic images representing a minor engaged in sexually explicit conduct. 3. For the purpose of paragraph 2 above, the term "minor" shall include all persons under 18 years of age. A Party may, however, require a lower age-limit, which shall be not less than 16 years.4. Each Party may reserve the right not to apply, in whole or in part, paragraphs 1, sub-paragraphs d. and e. and 2, sub-paragraphs b. and c.	**Control of Obscene and Indecent Article Ordinance Cap.390** S2 - "article" means any thing consisting of or containing material to be read or looked at or both read and looked at; any sound recording, and any film, video-tape, disc or other record of a picture or pictures S23 - displaying an indecent article – maximum sentence is a fine of $400,000 and to imprisonment for 12 months on the first conviction, and to a fine of $800,000 and to imprisonment for 12 months on a second or subsequent conviction **Prevention of Child Pornography Ordinance Cap.579** S2 - "child pornography" includes computer generated images or picture and data stored on a computer or by other electronic means S3 - any person who prints, makes, produces, reproduces, copies, publishes or imports any child pornography commits an offence

(continued)

Table 3 (continued)

	Convention	Hong Kong
Copyright Infringement Crimes	**Article 10** 1. Each Party shall adopt such legislative and other measures as may be necessary to establish as criminal offences under its domestic law the infringement of copyright, as defined under the law of that Party, pursuant to the obligations it has undertaken under the Paris Act of 24 July 1971 revising the Bern Convention for the Protection of Literary and Artistic Works, the Agreement on Trade-Related Aspects of Intellectual Property Rights and the WIPO Copyright Treaty, with the exception of any moral rights conferred by such conventions, where such acts are committed wilfully, on a commercial scale and by means of a computer system. 2. Each Party shall adopt such legislative and other measures as may be necessary to establish as criminal offences under its domestic law the infringement of related rights, as defined under the law of that Party, pursuant to the obligations it has undertaken under the International Convention for the Protection of Performers, Producers of Phonograms and Broadcasting Organisations (Rome Convention), the Agreement on Trade-Related Aspects of Intellectual Property Rights and the WIPO Performances and Phonograms Treaty, with the exception of any moral rights conferred by such conventions, where such acts are committed wilfully, on a commercial scale and by means of a computer system. 3. A Party may reserve the right not to impose criminal liability under paragraphs 1 and 2 of this article in limited circumstances, provided that other effective remedies are available and that such reservation does not derogate from the Party's international obligations set forth in the international instruments referred to in paragraphs 1 and 2 of this article.	**Copyright Ordinance Cap. 528** S118 - possessing, making or dealing with infringing articles is an offence S118(1)(f) - distributes (otherwise than for the purpose of, in the course of, or in connection with, any trade or business) to such an extent as to affect prejudicially the owner of the copyright

(continued)

Table 3 (continued)

	Convention	Hong Kong
	ADDITIONAL PROTOCOL TO THE CONVENTION ON CYBERCRIME	
Online Harassing	Article 3 – Dissemination of racist and xenophobic material through computer systems 1. Each Party shall adopt such legislative and other measures as may be necessary to establish as criminal offences under its domestic law, when committed intentionally and without right, the following conduct: distributing, or otherwise making available, racist and xenophobic material to the public through a computer system. 2. A Party may reserve the right not to attach criminal liability to conduct as defined by paragraph 1 of this article, where the material, as defined in Article 2, paragraph 1, advocates, promotes or incites discrimination that is not associated with hatred or violence, provided that other effective remedies are available. 3. Notwithstanding paragraph 2 of this article, a Party may reserve the right not to apply paragraph 1 to those cases of discrimination for which, due to established principles in its national legal system concerning freedom of expression, it cannot provide for effective remedies as referred to in the said paragraph 2.	**Race Discrimination Ordinance, Cap 602** S7 - "harass" = on the ground of race in an unwelcome conduct (oral/written) on anticipation that victime will be offended, humiliated or intimidated by that conduct. Creating a hostile/intimidating environment.
Hate Speech	Article 4 – Racist and xenophobic motivated threat 1. Each Party shall adopt such legislative and other measures as may be necessary to establish as criminal offences under its domestic law, when committed intentionally and without right, the following conduct: threatening, through a computer system, with the commission of a serious criminal offence as defined under its domestic law, (i) persons for the reason that they belong to a group, distinguished by race, colour, descent or national or ethnic origin, as well as religion, if used as a pretext for any of these factors, or (ii) a group of persons which is distinguished by any of these characteristics.	**Cimes Ordinance, Cap. 200**S9 - Seditious intention:(1)(c) to bring into hatred or contempt or to excite disaffection against administration of justice in Hong Kong (1)(d) to raise discontent or disaffection amongst inhabitants of Hong Kong (1)(e) to promote feelings of ill-will and enmity between different classes of population in Hong Kong (1)(f) to incite persons to violence (1)(g) to counsel disobedience to law or to any lawful order S10 - Offence = act with seditious intention, utters seditious words, print/publish/distribute/sells/displays/reproduce/import seditious materials

(continued)

Table 3 (continued)

	Convention	Hong Kong
Criminal Defamation	Article 5 – Racist and xenophobic motivated insult 1. Each Party shall adopt such legislative and other measures as may be necessary to establish as criminal offences under its domestic law, when committed intentionally and without right, the following conduct: insulting publicly, through a computer system, (i) persons for the reason that they belong to a group distinguished by race, colour, descent or national or ethnic origin, as well as religion, if used as a pretext for any of these factors; or (ii) a group of persons which is distinguished by any of these characteristics. 2. A Party may either: (a) require that the offence referred to in paragraph 1 of this article has the effect that the person or group of persons referred to in paragraph 1 is exposed to hatred, contempt or ridicule; or (b) reserve the right not to apply, in whole or in part, paragraph 1 of this article.	**Defamation Ordinance, Cap. 21** S2 - "broadcast" = publication for general reception within the definition of the Telecommunication Ordinance. Cap 106. S25 - Unintentional DefamationStatutory remedies possibly for ISPs as party of innocent dissemination where the author of defamatory remarks are made
Denial, gross minimisation, approval or justification of genocide or crimes against humanity	Article 6 – Denial, gross minimisation, approval or justification of genocide or crimes against humanity 1. Each Party shall adopt such legislative measures as may be necessary to establish the following conduct as criminal offences under its domestic law, when committed intentionally and without right: distributing or otherwise making available, through a computer system to the public, material which denies, grossly minimises, approves or justifies acts constituting genocide or crimes against humanity, as defined by international law and recognised as such by final and binding decisions of the International Military Tribunal, established by the London Agreement of 8 August 1945, or of any other international court established by relevant international instruments and whose jurisdiction is recognised by that Party. 2. A Party may either (a) require that the denial or the gross minimisation referred to in paragraph 1 of this article is committed with the intent to incite hatred, discrimination or violence against any individual or group of individuals, based on race, colour, descent or national or ethnic origin, as well as religion if used as a pretext for any of these factors, or otherwise (b) reserve the right not to apply, in whole or in part, paragraph 1 of this article.	NO KNOWN ORDINANCE IS SIMILAR TO / COMPLIES WITH THIS ARTICLE

(continued)

Table 4

	Convention	India
	Article 2 – Illegal access Each Party shall adopt such legislative and other measures as may be necessary to establish as criminal offences under its domestic law, when committed intentionally, the access to the whole or any part of a computer system without right. A Party may require that the offence be committed by infringing security measures, with the intent of obtaining computer data or other dishonest intent, or in relation to a computer system that is connected to another computer system.	**Section 66 (1) of The Information Technology Act, 2000** Cause wrongful loss or damage, destroys, deletes or alters any information residing in a computer resource = commits hacking **Section 72 of The Information Technology Act, 2000** Secured access to any electronic record, book, register, correspondence, information, document or other material without the consent of the person con
	Article 3 – Illegal interception Each Party shall adopt such legislative and other measures as may be necessary to establish as criminal offences under its domestic law, when committed intentionally, the interception without right, made by technical means, of non-public transmissions of computer data to, from or within a computer system, including electromagnetic emissions from a computer system carrying such computer data. A Party may require that the offence be committed with dishonest intent, or in relation to a computer system that is connected to another computer system.	**Section 70 of The Information Technology Act, 2000** Protection by government on declaration of 'protected system'
	Article 4 – Data interference 1. Each Party shall adopt such legislative and other measures as may be necessary to establish as criminal offences under its domestic law, when committed intentionally, the damaging, deletion, deterioration, alteration or suppression of computer data without right. 2. A Party may reserve the right to require that the conduct described in paragraph 1 result in serious harm.	**Section 66 (1) of The Information Technology Act, 2000** Cause wrongful loss or damage, destroys, deletes or alters any information residing in a computer resource = commits hacking
Offences against the confidentiality, integrity and availability of computer data and systems	**Article 5 – System interference** Each Party shall adopt such legislative and other measures as may be necessary to establish as criminal offences under its domestic law, when committed intentionally, the serious hindering without right of the functioning of a computer system by inputting, transmitting, damaging, deleting, deteriorating, altering or suppressing computer data.	**Section 65 of The Information Technology Act, 2000** Knowingly or intentionally conceals, destroys or alters computer resource

(continued)

Table 4 (continued)

	Convention	India
	Article 6 – Misuse of devices 1. Each Party shall adopt such legislative and other measures as may be necessary to establish as criminal offences under its domestic law, when committed intentionally and without right: (a) the production, sale, procurement for use, import, distribution or otherwise making available of: (i) a device, including a computer program, designed or adapted primarily for the purpose of committing any of the offences established in accordance with Articles 2 through 5; (ii) a computer password, access code, or similar data by which the whole or any part of a computer system is capable of being accessed, with intent that it be used for the purpose of committing any of the offences established in Articles 2 through 5; and (b) the possession of an item referred to in paragraphs (a, i or ii) above, with intent that it be used for the purpose of committing any of the offences established in Articles 2 through 5. A Party may require by law that a number of such items be possessed before criminal liability attaches. 2. This article shall not be interpreted as imposing criminal liability where the production, sale, procurement for use, import, distribution or otherwise making available or possession referred to in paragraph 1 of this article is not for the purpose of committing an offence established in accordance with Articles 2 through 5 of this Convention, such as for the authorised testing or protection of a computer system. 3. Each Party may reserve the right not to apply paragraph 1 of this article, provided that the reservation does not concern the sale, distribution or otherwise making available of the items referred to in paragraph 1, a, ii of this article.	**Section 67 of The Information Technology Act, 2000** Publishes or transmits or causes to be published in the electronic form, any material which is lascivious or appeals to the prurient interest or if its effect is such as to tend to deprave and corrupt persons who are likely, having regard to all relevant circumstances, to read, see or hear the matter contained or embodied in it
Forgery	**Article 7** Each Party shall adopt such legislative and other measures as may be necessary to establish as criminal offences under its domestic law, when committed intentionally and without right, the input, alteration, deletion, or suppression of computer data, resulting in inauthentic data with the intent that it be considered or acted upon for legal purposes as if it were authentic, regardless whether or not the data is directly readable and intelligible. A Party may require an intent to defraud, or similar dishonest intent, before criminal liability attaches.	**Section 71 of The Information Technology Act, 2000** Any misrepresentation to, or suppresses any material fact from, the Controller or the Certifying Authority for obtaining any licence or Digital Signature Certificate, as the case may be **Section 73 of The Information Technology Act, 2000** Publication of digital signature which are false in certain particulars

(continued)

Table 4 (continued)

	Convention	India
Online Fraud	**Article 8** Each Party shall adopt such legislative and other measures as may be necessary to establish as criminal offences under its domestic law, when committed intentionally and without right, the causing of a loss of property to another person by: (a) any input, alteration, deletion or suppression of computer data, (b) any interference with the functioning of a computer system, with fraudulent or dishonest intent of procuring, without right, an economic benefit for oneself or for another person.	**Section 74 of The Information Technology Act, 2000** Misrepresentation while obtaining, any license to act as a Certifying Authority or a digital signature certificate Sections 418, 419 and 420 of The Indian Penal CodeCheating to cause wrongful loss, by personation and dishonestly induces the person deceivedApplied in Sony.Sambandh.Com Case
Child Sexual Exploitation Materials	**Article 9** 1. Each Party shall adopt such legislative and other measures as may be necessary to establish as criminal offences under its domestic law, when committed intentionally and without right, the following conduct:(a) producing child pornography for the purpose of its distribution through a computer system; (b) offering or making available child pornography through a computer system; (c) distributing or transmitting child pornography through a computer system; (d) procuring child pornography through a computer system for oneself or for another person; (e) possessing child pornography in a computer system or on a computer-data storage medium. 2. For the purpose of paragraph 1 above, the term "child pornography" shall include pornographic material that visually depicts:(a) a minor engaged in sexually explicit conduct;(b) a person appearing to be a minor engaged in sexually explicit conduct;c) realistic images representing a minor engaged in sexually explicit conduct.3. For the purpose of paragraph 2 above, the term "minor" shall include all persons under 18 years of age. A Party may, however, require a lower age-limit, which shall be not less than 16 years. 4. Each Party may reserve the right not to apply, in whole or in part, paragraphs 1. sub-paragraphs d. and e, and 2. sub-paragraphs b. and c.	**Section 67 of The Information Technology Act, 2000** Publishes or transmits or causes to be published in the electronic form, any material which is lascivious or appeals to the prurient interest or if its effect is such as to tend to deprave and corrupt persons who are likely, having regard to all relevant circumstances, to read, see or hear the matter contained or embodied in it **Section 67B of The Information Technology Act, 2000 amended by Section 32 of Information Technology (Amendment) Act, 2008** Legislation is updated to expressly include provisions for child sexual exploitation material

(continued)

Table 4 (continued)

	Convention	India
Copyright Infringement Crimes	**Article 10** 1. Each Party shall adopt such legislative and other measures as may be necessary to establish as criminal offences under its domestic law the infringement of copyright, as defined under the law of that Party, pursuant to the obligations it has undertaken under the Paris Act of 24 July 1971 revising the Bern Convention for the Protection of Literary and Artistic Works, the Agreement on Trade-Related Aspects of Intellectual Property Rights and the WIPO Copyright Treaty, with the exception of any moral rights conferred by such conventions, where such acts are committed wilfully, on a commercial scale and by means of a computer system. 2. Each Party shall adopt such legislative and other measures as may be necessary to establish as criminal offences under its domestic law the infringement of related rights, as defined under the law of that Party, pursuant to the obligations it has undertaken under the International Convention for the Protection of Performers, Producers of Phonograms and Broadcasting Organisations (Rome Convention), the Agreement on Trade-Related Aspects of Intellectual Property Rights and the WIPO Performances and Phonograms Treaty, with the exception of any moral rights conferred by such conventions, where such acts are committed wilfully, on a commercial scale and by means of a computer system. 3. A Party may reserve the right not to impose criminal liability under paragraphs 1 and 2 of this article in limited circumstances, provided that other effective remedies are available and that such reservation does not derogate from the Party's international obligations set forth in the international instruments referred to in paragraphs 1 and 2 of this article.	**Section 71 of The Information Technology Act, 2000** Any misrepresentation to, or suppresses any material fact from, the Controller or the Certifying Authority for obtaining any licence or Digital Signature Certificate, as the case may beAapplied in Nasscom v. Ajay Sood & Others **Copyright Act, 1957** Section 3: 'publication' = making a work available to the public by issue of copies or by communicating the work to the publicSection 63: knowingly infringes or abets the infringement of

(continued)

Table 4 (continued)

	Convention	India
ADDITIONAL PROTOCOL TO THE CONVENTION ON CYBERCRIME		
Online Harassing	Article 3 – Dissemination of racist and xenophobic material through computer systems 1. Each Party shall adopt such legislative and other measures as may be necessary to establish as criminal offences under its domestic law, when committed intentionally and without right, the following conduct: distributing, or otherwise making available, racist and xenophobic material to the public through a computer system. 2. A Party may reserve the right not to attach criminal liability to conduct as defined by paragraph 1 of this article, where the material, as defined in Article 2, paragraph 1, advocates, promotes or incites discrimination that is not associated with hatred or violence, provided that other effective remedies are available. 3. Notwithstanding paragraph 2 of this article, a Party may reserve the right not to apply paragraph 1 to those cases of discrimination for which, due to established principles in its national legal system concerning freedom of expression, it cannot provide for effective remedies as referred to in the said paragraph 2.	**Section 67 of The Information Technology Act, 2000** Publishes or transmits or causes to be published in the electronic form, any material which is lascivious or appeals to the prurient interest or if its effect is such as to tend to deprave and corrupt persons who are likely, having regard to all relevant circumstances, to read, see or hear the matter contained or embodied in itApplied: State of Tamil Nadu Vs Suhas Katti
Hate Speech	Article 4 – Racist and xenophobic motivated threat 1. Each Party shall adopt such legislative and other measures as may be necessary to establish as criminal offences under its domestic law, when committed intentionally and without right, the following conduct: threatening, through a computer system, with the commission of a serious criminal offence as defined under its domestic law, (i) persons for the reason that they belong to a group, distinguished by race, colour, descent or national or ethnic origin, as well as religion, if used as a pretext for any of these factors, or (ii) a group of persons which is distinguished by any of these characteristics.	**Article 51A in The Constitution of India, 1949** Fundamental duty of Indian citizen to (h) develop scientific temper, humanism and the spirit of inquiry and reform and (i) to safeguard public property and to abjure violence There is no regulation specifically for online hate speech.

(continued)

Table 4 (continued)

	Convention	India
Criminal Defamation	Article 5 – Racist and xenophobic motivated insult 1. Each Party shall adopt such legislative and other measures as may be necessary to establish as criminal offences under its domestic law, when committed intentionally and without right, the following conduct: insulting publicly, through a computer system, (i) persons for the reason that they belong to a group distinguished by race, colour, descent or national or ethnic origin, as well as religion, if used as a pretext for any of these factors; or (ii) a group of persons which is distinguished by any of these characteristics. 2. A Party may either: (a) require that the offence referred to in paragraph 1 of this article has the effect that the person or group of persons referred to in paragraph 1 is exposed to hatred, contempt or ridicule; or (b) reserve the right not to apply, in whole or in part, paragraph 1 of this article.	**Section 67 of The Information Technology Act, 2000** Publishes or transmits or causes to be published in the electronic form, any material which is lascivious or appeals to the prurient interest or if its effect is such as to tend to deprave and corrupt persons who are likely, having regard to all relevant circumstances, to read, see or hear the matter contained or embodied in it Applied: SMC Pneumatics (India) Pvt. Ltd. v. Jogesh Kwatra
Denial, gross minimisation, approval or justification of genocide or crimes against humanity	**Article 6 – Denial, gross minimisation, approval or justification of genocide or crimes against humanity** 1. Each Party shall adopt such legislative measures as may be necessary to establish the following conduct as criminal offences under its domestic law, when committed intentionally and without right:distributing or otherwise making available, through a computer system to the public, material which denies, grossly minimises, approves or justifies acts constituting genocide or crimes against humanity, as defined by international law and recognised as such by final and binding decisions of the International Military Tribunal, established by the London Agreement of 8 August 1945, or of any other international court established by relevant international instruments and whose jurisdiction is recognised by that Party. 2. A Party may either(a) require that the denial or the gross minimisation referred to in paragraph 1 of this article is committed with the intent to incite hatred, discrimination or violence against any individual or group of individuals, based on race, colour, descent or national or ethnic origin, as well as religion if used as a pretext for any of these factors, or otherwise (b) reserve the right not to apply, in whole or in part, paragraph 1 of this article.	**NO KNOWN LEGISLATION IS SIMILAR TO / COMPLIES WITH THIS ARTICLE**

Table 5

	Convention	Japan
Offences against the confidentiality, integrity and availability of computer data and systems	**Article 2 – Illegal access** Each Party shall adopt such legislative and other measures as may be necessary to establish as criminal offences under its domestic law, when committed intentionally, the access to the whole or any part of a computer system without right. A Party may require that the offence be committed by infringing security measures, with the intent of obtaining computer data or other dishonest intent, or in relation to a computer system that is connected to another computer system.	**Article 1 of the Unauthorised Computer Access Law (Act No. 128 of 1999)** purpose = prohibiting acts of unauthorised computer access to prevent computer-related crimes and to maintain order **Article 3 of the Unauthorised Computer Access Law (Act No. 128 of 1999)** types of unauthorised computer access
	Article 3 – Illegal interception Each Party shall adopt such legislative and other measures as may be necessary to establish as criminal offences under its domestic law, when committed intentionally, the interception without right, made by technical means, of non-public transmissions of computer data to, from or within a computer system, including electromagnetic emissions from a computer system carrying such computer data. A Party may require that the offence be committed with dishonest intent, or in relation to a computer system that is connected to another computer system.	**as above Article 3 Article 3 of the Unauthorised Computer Access Law (Act No. 128 of 1999)**
	Article 4 – Data interference 1. Each Party shall adopt such legislative and other measures as may be necessary to establish as criminal offences under its domestic law, when committed intentionally, the damaging, deletion, deterioration, alteration or suppression of computer data without right. 2. A Party may reserve the right to require that the conduct described in paragraph 1 result in serious harm.	**Article 7-2 of the Penal Code (Act No.45 of 1907)** Definition of 'electromagnetic record' = any record produced by electronic, magnetic or any other means unrecognised by natural perceptive functions and is used for data-processing by a computer **Article 258, 259 and 264 of the Penal Code (Act No.45 of 1907)** pertaining to destruction of electromagnetic record
	Article 5 – System interference Each Party shall adopt such legislative and other measures as may be necessary to establish as criminal offences under its domestic law, when committed intentionally, the serious hindering without right of the functioning of a computer system by inputting, transmitting, damaging, deleting, deteriorating, altering or suppressing computer data.	**Article 234-2 of the Penal Code (Act No.45 of 1907)** interfering with the operation of the computer by damaging such computer or any data, by inputting false data or giving unauthorised commands or by any other means

(continued)

Table 5 (continued)

Convention	Japan
Article 6 – Misuse of devices 1. Each Party shall adopt such legislative and other measures as may be necessary to establish as criminal offences under its domestic law, when committed intentionally and without right(a) the production, sale, procurement for use, import, distribution or otherwise making available of: (i) a device, including a computer program, designed or adapted primarily for the purpose of committing any of the offences established in accordance with Articles 2 through 5; (ii) a computer password, access code, or similar data by which the whole or any part of a computer system is capable of being accessed, with intent that it be used for the purpose of committing any of the offences established in Articles 2 through 5; and (b) the possession of an item referred to in paragraphs a.i or ii above, with intent that it be used for the purpose of committing any of the offences established in Articles 2 through 5. A Party may require by law that a number of such items be possessed before criminal liability attaches. 2. This article shall not be interpreted as imposing criminal liability where the production, sale, procurement for use, import, distribution or otherwise making available or possession referred to in paragraph 1 of this article is not for the purpose of committing an offence established in accordance with Articles 2 through 5 of this Convention, such as for the authorised testing or protection of a computer system.3. Each Party may reserve the right not to apply paragraph 1 of this article, provided that the reservation does not concern the sale, distribution or otherwise making available of the items referred to in paragraph 1 a.ii of this article.	**Draft Law for Partial Amendment of Criminal Code in Response to Growing Criminal Internationalization and Organization and More Sophisticated Information Processing Bill before the Diet** NO RELEVANT OFFENCE AT THE MOMENT
Forgery	
Article 7 Each Party shall adopt such legislative and other measures as may be necessary to establish as criminal offences under its domestic law, when committed intentionally and without right, the input, alteration, deletion, or suppression of computer data, resulting in inauthentic data with the intent that it be considered or acted upon for legal purposes as if it were authentic, regardless whether or not the data is directly readable and intelligible. A Party may require an intent to defraud, or similar dishonest intent, before criminal liability attaches.	**Article 161 of the Penal Code (Act No.45 of 1907)** with intent, unlawfully create without due authorisation data for use in such improper administration

(continued)

Table 5 (continued)

	Convention	Japan
Online Fraud	**Article 8** Each Party shall adopt such legislative and other measures as may be necessary to establish as criminal offences under its domestic law, when committed intentionally and without right, the causing of a loss of property to another person by: (a) any input, alteration, deletion or suppression of computer data, (b) any interference with the functioning of a computer system, with fraudulent or dishonest intent of procuring, without right, an economic benefit for oneself or for another person.	**Article 246-2 of the Penal Code (Act No.45 of 1907)** obtains or causes another to obtain a profit by creating or putting into use a false electromagnetic record relating to acquisition, loss or alteration of property rights by inputting false data or giving unauthorised commands to a computer. **Article 250 of the Penal Code (Act No.45 of 1907)** Attempt of the above crime applies as well
Child Sexual Exploitation Materials	**Article 9** 1. Each Party shall adopt such legislative and other measures as may be necessary to establish as criminal offences under its domestic law, when committed intentionally and without right, the following conduct: (a) producing child pornography for the purpose of its distribution through a computer system; (b) offering or making available child pornography through a computer system; (c) distributing or transmitting child pornography through a computer system;d) procuring child pornography through a computer system for oneself or for another person; (e) possessing child pornography in a computer system or on a computer-data storage medium. 2. For the purpose of paragraph 1 above, the term "child pornography" shall include pornographic material that visually depicts: (a) a minor engaged in sexually explicit conduct; (b) a person appearing to be a minor engaged in sexually explicit conduct; (c) realistic images representing a minor engaged in sexually explicit conduct. 3. For the purpose of paragraph 2 above, the term "minor" shall include all persons under 18 years of age. A Party may, however, require a lower age-limit, which shall be not less than 16 years. 4. Each Party may reserve the right not to apply, in whole or in part, paragraphs 1. sub-paragraphs d. and e, and 2. sub-paragraphs b. and c.	**Article 175 of the Penal Code (Act No.45 of 1907)** distributes, sells or display in public an obscene document, drawing or other objects **Article 7 of the Act on Punishment of Activities Relating to Child Prostitution and Child Pornography, and the Protection of Children (Act No. 52 of 1999)** distributes, produces, possess, transports, imports to or exports from Japan child sexual exploitation materials

(continued)

Table 5 (continued)

	Convention	Japan
Copyright Infringement Crimes	**Article 10** 1. Each Party shall adopt such legislative and other measures as may be necessary to establish as criminal offences under its domestic law the infringement of copyright, as defined under the law of that Party, pursuant to the obligations it has undertaken under the Paris Act of 24 July 1971 revising the Bern Convention for the Protection of Literary and Artistic Works, the Agreement on Trade-Related Aspects of Intellectual Property Rights and the WIPO Copyright Treaty, with the exception of any moral rights conferred by such conventions, where such acts are committed wilfully, on a commercial scale and by means of a computer system. 2. Each Party shall adopt such legislative and other measures as may be necessary to establish as criminal offences under its domestic law the infringement of related rights, as defined under the law of that Party, pursuant to the obligations it has undertaken under the International Convention for the Protection of Performers, Producers of Phonograms and Broadcasting Organisations (Rome Convention), the Agreement on Trade-Related Aspects of Intellectual Property Rights and the WIPO Performances and Phonograms Treaty, with the exception of any moral rights conferred by such conventions, where such acts are committed wilfully, on a commercial scale and by means of a computer system. 3. A Party may reserve the right not to impose criminal liability under paragraphs 1 and 2 of this article in limited circumstances, provided that other effective remedies are available and that such reservation does not derogate from the Party's international obligations set forth in the international instruments referred to in paragraphs 1 and 2 of this article.	**Article 119 of Copyright Act (Act No. 48 of 1970)** infringement of the copyright, right of publication or neighbouring rights shall be punishable **Article 121 of Copyright Act (Act No. 48 of 1970)** distribution of reproduction of a work who is not the author shall be punishable **Article 121(2) of Copyright Act (Act No. 48 of 1970)** makes, distributes or possesses for distribution copies of commercial phonograms reproduced from any of the following commercial phonograms **Article 123 of Copyright Act (Act No. 48 of 1970)** rosecution shall take place only upon the complaint of the injured person **Article 124 of Copyright Act (Act No. 48 of 1970)** offending employees of violated legal person or business shall be punishable by fine **The revision to the Copyright Law cleared the Education, Culture and Science Committee of the House of Councilors on 22 June 2012, to take effect on 1 October 2012** penalising Internet users for downloading pirated music and video files (no relevant English translation available)

(continued)

Table 5 (continued)

	Convention	Japan
ADDITIONAL PROTOCOL TO THE CONVENTION ON CYBERCRIME		

Overarching legislation that applies:Article 3(1) of the Act on the Limitation of Liability for Damages of SpecifiedTelecommunications Service Providers (2001) indemnity provided to service providers for any infringement occurs where the provider had distributed a third party communication, unless (a) feasible to prevent transmission of the infringing communication/s and (b) knowledge of infringement by distribution or knowledge of information in the offending communication
Act on International Assistance in Investigation and OtherRelated Matters (Act No. 69 of 1980, in effect from June 2012)
Methods of seizure and criminal procedure laws

Online Harassing

Article 3 – Dissemination of racist and xenophobic material through computer systems

1. Each Party shall adopt such legislative and other measures as may be necessary to establish as criminal offences under its domestic law, when committed intentionally and without right, the following conduct: distributing, or otherwise making available, racist and xenophobic material to the public through a computer system.

2. A Party may reserve the right not to attach criminal liability to conduct as defined by paragraph 1 of this article, where the material, as defined in Article 2, paragraph 1, advocates, promotes or incites discrimination that is not associated with hatred or violence, provided that other effective remedies are available.

3. Notwithstanding paragraph 2 of this article, a Party may reserve the right not to apply paragraph 1 to those cases of discrimination for which, due to established principles in its national legal system concerning freedom of expression, it cannot provide for effective remedies as referred to in the said paragraph 2.

Law on Proscribing Stalking Behavior and Assisting Victims (2000)
General national law on stalking

(continued)

Table 5 (continued)

	Convention	Japan
Hate Speech	Article 4 – Racist and xenophobic motivated threat 1. Each Party shall adopt such legislative and other measures as may be necessary to establish as criminal offences under its domestic law, when committed intentionally and without right, the following conduct: threatening, through a computer system, with the commission of a serious criminal offence as defined under its domestic law, (i) persons for the reason that they belong to a group, distinguished by race, colour, descent or national or ethnic origin, as well as religion, if used as a pretext for any of these factors, or (ii) a group of persons which is distinguished by any of these characteristics.	**Article 231 of the Penal Code (Act No.45 of 1907)** General misdemeanor for insulting
Criminal Defamation	Article 5 – Racist and xenophobic motivated insult 1. Each Party shall adopt such legislative and other measures as may be necessary to establish as criminal offences under its domestic law, when committed intentionally and without right, the following conduct: insulting publicly, through a computer system, (i) persons for the reason that they belong to a group distinguished by race, colour, descent or national or ethnic origin, as well as religion, if used as a pretext for any of these factors; or (ii) a group of persons which is distinguished by any of these characteristics. 2. A Party may either: (a) require that the offence referred to in paragraph 1 of this article has the effect that the person or group of persons referred to in paragraph 1 is exposed to hatred, contempt or ridicule; or (b) reserve the right not to apply, in whole or in part, paragraph 1 of this article.	**Article 230 of the Penal Code (Act No.45 of 1907)** General defamation protection

(continued)

Table 6 (continued)

Convention	UK
Article 6 – Misuse of devices	**S2 of the Computer Misuse Act 1990** intention to secure unauthorised access to computer materials + intent to commit/facilitiate the commission of further offences
1. Each Party shall adopt such legislative and other measures as may be necessary to establish as criminal offences under its domestic law, when committed intentionally and without right:(a) the production, sale, procurement for use, import, distribution or otherwise making available of: (i) a device, including a computer program, designed or adapted primarily for the purpose of committing any of the offences established in accordance with Articles 2 through 5; (ii) a computer password, access code, or similar data by which the whole or any part of a computer system is capable of being accessed, with intent that it be used for the purpose of committing any of the offences established in Articles 2 through 5; and (b) the possession of an item referred to in paragraphs a. i or ii above, with intent that it be used for the purpose of committing any of the offences established in Articles 2 through 5. A Party may require by law that a number of such items be possessed before criminal liability attaches. 2. This article shall not be interpreted as imposing criminal liability where the production, sale, procurement for use, import, distribution or otherwise making available or possession referred to in paragraph 1 of this article is not for the purpose of committing an offence established in accordance with Articles 2 through 5 of this Convention, such as for the authorised testing or protection of a computer system.3. Each Party may reserve the right not to apply paragraph 1 of this article, provided that the reservation does not concern the sale, distribution or otherwise making available of the items referred to in paragraph 1 a.ii of this article.	

(continued)

Table 6 (continued)

	Convention	UK
Forgery	**Article 7** Each Party shall adopt such legislative and other measures as may be necessary to establish as criminal offences under its domestic law, when committed intentionally and without right, the input, alteration, deletion, or suppression of computer data, resulting in inauthentic data with the intent that it be considered or acted upon for legal purposes as if it were authentic, regardless whether or not the data is directly readable and intelligible. A Party may require an intent to defraud, or similar dishonest intent, before criminal liability attaches.	**Computer Misuse Act and s1 of the Forgery and Counterfeiting Act 1981** false instrument to induce somebody to accept it as genuine.
Online Fraud	**Article 8** Each Party shall adopt such legislative and other measures as may be necessary to establish as criminal offences under its domestic law, when committed intentionally and without right, the causing of a loss of property to another person by: (a) any input, alteration, deletion or suppression of computer data, (b) any interference with the functioning of a computer system, with fraudulent or dishonest intent of procuring, without right, an economic benefit for oneself or for another person.	**s6 of The Fraud Act 2006** possession or in control of an article for use in the course of or in connection with any fraud. 'Article' = can construed as the use of equipment eg computers, etc. **The National Fraud Reporting Centre: Action Fraud**http://www.actionfraud.police.uk/

(continued)

Table 6 (continued)

Convention	UK
ADDITIONAL PROTOCOL TO THE CONVENTION ON CYBERCRIME	
Online Harassing Article 3 – Dissemination of racist and xenophobic material through computer systems 1. Each Party shall adopt such legislative and other measures as may be necessary to establish as criminal offences under its domestic law, when committed intentionally and without right, the following conduct: distributing, or otherwise making available, racist and xenophobic material to the public through a computer system. 2. A Party may reserve the right not to attach criminal liability to conduct as defined by paragraph 1 of this article, where the material, as defined in Article 2, paragraph 1, advocates, promotes or incites discrimination that is not associated with hatred or violence, provided that other effective remedies are available. 3. Notwithstanding paragraph 2 of this article, a Party may reserve the right not to apply paragraph 1 to those cases of discrimination for which, due to established principles in its national legal system concerning freedom of expression, it cannot provide for effective remedies as referred to in the said paragraph 2.	**s127 of the Communications Act 2003** sending of improper messages. 'grossly offensive' test used. **s2 of Protection from Harassment Act 1997** course of conduct that amounts to harassment of another **s4 of Protection from Harassment Act 1997** course of conduct causes another to fear that violence will be used against him/her
Hate Speech Article 4 – Racist and xenophobic motivated threat 1. Each Party shall adopt such legislative and other measures as may be necessary to establish as criminal offences under its domestic law, when committed intentionally and without right, the following conduct: threatening, through a computer system, with the commission of a serious criminal offence as defined under its domestic law, (i) persons for the reason that they belong to a group, distinguished by race, colour, descent or national or ethnic origin, as well as religion, if used as a pretext for any of these factors, or (ii) a group of persons which is distinguished by any of these characteristics.	**s2 of the Malicious Communications Act 1988** indecent, grossly offensive or which convey a threat, and where there is an intent to cause distress or anxiety to the recipient. **Part III of the Public Order Act 1986:** addressing of racist materials

(continued)

Table 6 (continued)

	Convention	UK
Criminal Defamation	Article 5 – Racist and xenophobic motivated insult 1. Each Party shall adopt such legislative and other measures as may be necessary to establish as criminal offences under its domestic law, when committed intentionally and without right, the following conduct: insulting publicly, through a computer system, (i) persons for the reason that they belong to a group distinguished by race, colour, descent or national or ethnic origin, as well as religion, if used as a pretext for any of these factors; or (ii) a group of persons which is distinguished by any of these characteristics. 2. A Party may either: (a) require that the offence referred to in paragraph 1 of this article has the effect that the person or group of persons referred to in paragraph 1 is exposed to hatred, contempt or ridicule; or (b) reserve the right not to apply, in whole or in part, paragraph 1 of this article.	**Defamation Act 1996** Defamation Bill 2012-13 at 2nd reading before the House of Lords on 9 October 2012 to update on the requirement of serious harm, the defences, the single publication rule, jurisdiction, trial without jury, removal of statements from websites, special damages regarding slander and the difference between 'publish' and 'statement'
Denial, gross minimisation, approval or justification of genocide or crimes against humanity	**Article 6 – Denial, gross minimisation, approval or justification of genocide or crimes against humanity** 1. Each Party shall adopt such legislative measures as may be necessary to establish the following conduct as criminal offences under its domestic law, when committed intentionally and without right: distributing or otherwise making available, through a computer system to the public, material which denies, grossly minimises, approves or justifies acts constituting genocide or crimes against humanity, as defined by international law and recognised as such by final and binding decisions of the International Military Tribunal, established by the London Agreement of 8 August 1945, or of any other international court established by relevant international instruments and whose jurisdiction is recognised by that Party. 2. A Party may either (a) require that the denial or the gross minimisation referred to in paragraph 1 of this article is committed with the intent to incite hatred, discrimination or violence against any individual or group of individuals, based on race, colour, descent or national or ethnic origin, as well as religion if used as a pretext for any of these factors, or otherwise(b) reserve the right not to apply, in whole or in part, paragraph 1 of this article.	**s127 of the Communications Act 2003** sending of improper messages. 'grossly offensive' test used. **s2 of the Malicious Communications Act 1988** indecent, grossly offensive or which convey a threat, and where there is an intent to cause distress or anxiety to the recipient.

References

1. Plfeeger C, Pfleeger S (2007) Security in computing. 4th edn Prentice Hall, NJ, p 4
2. Gutman P (2011) The commercial Malware industry. Available at www.cs.auckland.ac.nz/~p gut001/pubs/malware_biz.pdf. Last Accessed 4 Feb 2011
3. Clarke R (2009) Categories of Malware. Available at http://www.rogerclarke.com/II/MalCat-0909.html. Last Accessed 7 Feb 2011)
4. Dunham K, Melnick J (2009) Malicious bots. CRC Press, Boca Raton, p 54
5. Dunham K, Melnick J (2009) Malicious bots: an inside look into the cyber-criminal underground of the internet. CRC Press, Boca Raton, p 132
6. Gaaster L (2008) GNSO Council issues report on FastFlux hosting. Available at http://www.i cann.org
7. Barakat A, Khattab S (2010) "A comparative study of traditional Botnets versus super-Botnet" in INFOSEC 2010
8. Vogt R, Aycock J, Jacobson M (2007) Army of Botnets Network And Distributed System Security Symposium (ISOC). Available at http://pages.cpsc.ucalgary.ca/~aycock/papers/ndss07.pdf
9. Wouters P (2009) Defending your DNS in a Post-Kaminsky World Black Hat Computer Security Conference. Available at http://www.blackhat.com/presentations/bh-dc-09-Wouters/BlackHat-DC-09-Wouters-Post-Dan-Kaminsky-slides.pdf
10. Clarke R (2004) Peer-to-peer (P2P)—an overview. Available at http://rogerclarke.com/EC/P2POview.html
11. Oram A (ed) (2001) Peer-to-peer: harnessing the power of disruptive technologies. O'Reily & Associates, Sebastopol
12. Samuels A (2004) Hacktivism and the future of political participation, PhD Thesis, Harvard